THE GREAT DEPRESSION IN AMERICAN HISTORY

David K. Fremon

Enslow Publishers, Inc.

44 Fadem Road   PO Box 38
Box 699   Aldershot
Springfield, NJ 07081 Hants GU12 6BP
USA   UK

Dedicated to all reference librarians, who make a writer's life so much easier.

Library of Congress Cataloging-in-Publication Data

Fremon, David K.
      The Great Depression in American history / David K.Fremon.
          p. cm. — (In American history)
      Includes bibliographical references and index.
      Summary: Describes the history surrounding the Great Depression,
highlighting the causes and key figures.
      ISBN 0-89490-881-2
      1. Depressions—1929—United States—Juvenile literature. 2. United
States—Economic conditions—1918-1945—Juvenile literature. 3. New
Deal, 1933–1939—Juvenile literature. 4. Roosevelt, Franklin D. (Franklin
Delano), 1882-1945—Juvenile literature. [1. Depressions—1929.
2. New Deal, 1933–1939. 3. United States—Economic conditions—
1918-1945.] I. Title. II. Series.
HC106.3.F69 1997
338.5'42—dc20   96-34289
                                                                              CIP
                                                                              AC

Printed in the United States of America.

10 9 8 7 6 5 4 3 2 1

Illustration Credits: Farm Service Administration, pp. 7, 29, 30, 34, 53, 59, 70, 72, 74, 75, 76, 100, 104, 106, 108, 117, 118; Library of Congress, pp. 19, 39, 46, 65, 98; Karl M. Rivera, pp. 55, 103; Larry Esposito, p. 57; The Chicago Public Library, Sulzer Regional Library, p. 58.

Cover Illustrations: Farm Service Administration.

★ CONTENTS ★

"WALL STREET LAYS AN EGG"

Early rising New York residents witnessed an eerie morning spectacle on October 28, 1929. The sky was dark with thousands of blackbirds descending on the heart of the city. The birds landed at the Wall Street financial district, spent half an hour eating every bit of available food, then flew away as suddenly and unexpectedly as they had arrived. Nearly a hundred of the birds, too starved or weary to make the flight, were left behind and died.

The birds might have been an omen of dire events to come. One day later, Wall Street would be the setting for another bizarre event—a tragedy that would touch people throughout the United States and the world.

Watching Their Fate

Thousands of men and women thronged the streets of downtown New York on the morning of Tuesday, October 29, 1929. The city's police chief sent out extra detectives and uniformed officers to handle the large gathering. They were not crowding at the doors of a sports arena or an entertainment hall. Instead, they tried to enter the New York Stock Exchange building.

These were grim, curious, downhearted, and sometimes angry spectators. They came to see if the stock market would collapse. Many waited from more than curiosity. They had invested money in stocks that were bought and sold at the stock exchange. If the stocks sold at higher prices, they made money. But if stock prices fell, they lost. Some already had seen their investments disappear on the previous "Black Thursday," October 24. Others waited to see if they would go home bankrupt.

The anxiety was repeated in big cities and small towns. Investors, their hearts beating in fear, jammed into local stockbrokers' offices and crowded around the ticker machine. This electronic messenger gave the investors news of their economic fate. Very few got the results they wished for; more received the message they feared.

The Crash

As always, the trading began promptly at 10:00 A.M., Eastern Time. From the opening gong, the market was a disaster. More than 3 million shares changed hands in the first thirty minutes. Nearly all transactions were sales; no one was buying any stock.

On Black Thursday, some of New York's leading financiers had bought up stock in the afternoon. They had stemmed a selling spree that began earlier that day. By doing so, they had kept the market from total ruin.

Today, however, no one made such a move. Trying to stop this selling spree, someone remarked, would be like "trying to stem the falls of Niagara."[1]

Instead, big investors dumped blocks of fifty thousand shares. These were shares of stock from the nation's major companies: Chrysler Motors, General Electric, International Telephone and Telegraph, Standard Oil of New Jersey. As the market prices of these stocks plummeted, sellers received only a fraction of their buying price in return. General Electric, which started the day costing $245 a share, fell to $211. RCA plunged from one hundred dollars to a mere twenty-six dollars. Blue Ridge Corporation, which started August at one hundred dollars, plummeted to three dollars a share. In one brokerage house, an office boy

A Depression era woman, uncertain of her fate, comforts her two children.

offered one dollar per share for White Sewing Machine stock, which had sold for forty-eight dollars the day before. The desperate brokers sold it to him.[2]

When the larger investors sold out, others panicked. Brokers, trying to avoid bankruptcy for themselves, sold the stock of smaller investors. After the brokers took their fees, the small investors often were left with nothing. For many, the money placed in the stock market represented their life savings.

By noon, more than 8 million shares had been traded. Shortly afterward, the governing committee of the stock exchange met in the building's basement. As panicked brokers frantically sold their clients' stocks upstairs, the committee debated what it should do. The members finally decided to stay open and hope for a miracle.

That miracle never happened. Late-afternoon buying raised the market prices slightly, but the overall totals were devastating. Sales outscored purchases by $9 billion. In stock exchanges throughout the country, losses amounted to $15 billion. Official records noted that 16.4 million shares of stock were sold. Yet sales were so frantic that many transactions went unrecorded. The real total might have been closer to 20 or 25 million shares.

Some tried to put a cheerful face on the Wall Street disaster. *The New York Times* headline of the following day read "Rally at Close Cheers Brokers." Ninety-year-old billionaire John D. Rockefeller tried to show his confidence in the market the next day by offering to buy huge quantities of stock. Comedian Eddie Cantor quipped, "Sure, who else had any money left?"[3] The show business newspaper *Variety* had a blunt headline: "WALL ST. LAYS AN EGG."[4]

For many stock investors, October 29, 1929, was the worst day of their lives. One distraught broker ran from the trading floor "screaming like a lunatic."[5] He ran outside the building, where ten thousand observers watched the market failure in stunned silence. Those extra police were not needed. The crowd on Wall Street behaved more like zombies than revolutionaries.

In the case of some investors, October 29, 1929, was the last day of their lives. Speculators crawled onto ledges of their skyscraper buildings, then leaped to death on the streets below. Others swallowed poison or inhaled deadly gas. A Kansas City man, after having lost a fortune, told a friend: "Tell the boys I can't pay them what I owe them." Then he shot himself.[6]

October 29, 1929, became known as "Black Tuesday," or the day of the Crash. It marked the unofficial start of an era known as the Great Depression. Not everyone was hit immediately by economic woes. But few would escape the effects of the nation's crisis. Most Americans had become used to prosperity in the 1920s. Soon hunger, poverty, and unemployment would be their constant companions.

2

"THE BUSINESS OF AMERICA IS BUSINESS"

Leaders from Germany and the Allied nations gathered at a railroad car in a French forest. The mood was serious as they discussed Germany's surrender. On November 11, 1918, they signed a peace agreement. The four-year-long war, World War I, the bloodiest war in history, was over.

In the United States, people were anything but somber. Parades and welcome-home celebrations marked the end of the war. Americans had entered the conflict in 1917 reluctantly. With America's help, Britain and France had been able to triumph over the Germans.

Now Americans could get back to business. They wanted to stay out of foreign affairs. Congress ignored President Woodrow Wilson's pleas to join the newly-formed League of Nations. In 1920, Republican Warren Harding was elected president with the slogan "Back to Normalcy." Americans desired normalcy. They wished to live peacefully, party, and make money.

The Roaring Twenties

America more than prospered during the 1920s. The country went through the greatest economic boom the world had ever seen. Businesses thrived. Many companies passed their good fortune on to their workers. They sponsored recreational facilities and athletic teams. Some gave workers housing, insurance, and the chance to buy company stock.

Disposable income grew for most people. The average American now could buy more than necessities. He or she took advantage of that opportunity. Earlier generations encouraged savings. In the 1920s, saving money was almost considered unpatriotic.

Technological advances created new consumer goods. Vacuum cleaners, electric fans, toasters, and other luxury items became available to average Americans. Millions also bought the latest communications device, the radio.

Messages from the radio encouraged further consumption. Advertising became a major force in the 1920s. Through radio, newspapers, and magazines, companies reached customers in record numbers. They persuaded customers of the importance of the latest goods. A housewife did not just want a refrigerator or washing machine—she *needed* it.

Advertising affected the economy in another way. Companies who advertised wisely saw rapid growth in their business. Those who did not often went bankrupt. As a result, fewer but larger companies controlled the American economy. By 1929, two hundred corporations controlled nearly half of American industry.

Few Americans bought these items with available cash. Instead, they used the credit system. Stores sold items for a small—or sometimes no—down payment.

Buyers then paid the store a few dollars at a time, over a period of months. Customers got the goods right away. But the constant credit payments meant that few people saved much money. Those that did have extra money found a new place to invest it: the stock market.

The Stock Market

Businesses try to make money. Workers with money to spare often use those funds to try and make more money. These two groups come together in the stock market.

If a business is successful, it may seek more money so it can expand. One way to gain such money is by selling part of the company (stock) to outsiders. Each portion is known as a share of stock. Investors may buy (and later sell) this stock. Doctors, teachers, and plumbers invest in stocks. So do major financial institutions such as banks. Companies may use some profits to invest in other companies.

Buyers and sellers do not deal directly with the companies for stock. Instead, they conduct business at markets known as stock exchanges. Investment bankers buy all available stock from a company. They sell it or buy it back at the exchange. Investors likewise do not deal directly with the stock exchange. They act through agents known as brokers, who collect a fee from every stock sale. Brokers willing to buy stock meet with brokers willing to sell. They agree on a price, and that sale price is the stock's market price. If trading partners cannot be found, a specialist representing the company buys or sells the requested stock.

The stock market offers no guarantees. If investors are interested in buying stock in a company, the value of that stock increases. This means more potential money for the investor and more money for the company. If fewer people are interested, the price falls. The investor loses money by selling the stock for less than he or she paid for it. The company loses because unsold stock or stock at lesser value means less money for other investments. Investors who buy stocks at low prices and sell at high ones can make a fortune. Those who unwisely put their money into falling stocks may lose their money.

Several American cities have stock exchanges. The largest, the New York Stock Exchange, is located on Wall Street in New York City. Before World War I, many Americans saw "Wall Street" as the home of greedy tycoons whose actions kept many people poor. In the 1920s, these same Americans had a different view. Now that they had some money, they wanted a share of the money made in owning stocks. The wealthy few still owned most stocks. But teachers, mail carriers, secretaries, and shopkeepers now began to own stocks. "Taxi drivers told you what to buy," millionaire financier Bernard Baruch recalled. "The shoeshine boy could give you a summary of the day's financial news."[1]

Most stock advisors used one word: "buy." Stock prices rose throughout the decade as more and more people invested in RCA or U.S. Steel. Since people continually invested, stock prices kept rising. Corporate directors and chauffeurs alike welcomed the news. The stock market was making them rich—or so they thought.

Crumbling Blocks

More Americans were riding cars, buying appliances, and investing in stocks than ever before. They danced the Charleston, watched Babe Ruth slug home runs, and drank outlawed liquor at illegal taverns called "speakeasies." To many, the 1920s seemed like a never-ending party.

But underneath this prosperity lurked serious economic problems. If no one dealt with these problems, the country could face financial ruin.

Distribution of wealth was far from equal. The rich were getting richer. The richest one tenth of one percent of Americans had as much combined income as the poorest 42 percent of Americans. While the average disposable income increased 9 percent during the 1920s, the richest one percent saw a 75 percent increase. Less than 3 percent of Americans had two thirds of the country's savings, while 80 percent of Americans had no savings at all.[2]

Productivity rose faster than incomes during the 1920s. This meant that factories were producing more goods than Americans could buy. These surplus goods could not be sold overseas. European countries were still devastated by World War I. Most had huge war debts to repay to the United States, which became the world's leading creditor nation. Many countries in Africa, Asia, and Latin America were either European colonies or underdeveloped independent nations. Most of their citizens lacked the money needed to buy American goods.

Farmers did not share in the overall prosperity. For much of the 1920s, they suffered. Farmers had increased production to supply the Allies with food during World War I. After the war, Europeans no longer needed this American help. Yet American farms did not cut back on production. As new machines such as tractors became available, farmers could produce more crops using fewer people. But Americans could not eat everything the farmers produced. The farmers were growing too much food. Because of this over-production, farm prices tumbled. While their profits became less and less, their debts remained the same or increased. Thus farmers were poorer than ever.

Many investors bought their stocks on margin. This meant they paid only a small percentage of the stock's value when they purchased it. Someone buying a hundred dollars worth of stock, for example, might pay a stockbroker only ten dollars immediately. In return, the broker wanted collateral, some kind of assurance that the buyer had the money to pay his or her debt.

Often, the buyer used the stock itself as collateral. He or she promised to turn the stock over to the broker to cover money owed on it. If the value of the stock continued to rise, this would be no problem. But if the stock prices ever fell, the stock would be worth less money, and the collateral would be less valuable.

Banks took an active part in the stock market. Many used depositors' money to finance stock purchases. In 1928, there were $5 billion worth of bank loans. Much of this money was lent to speculators who gambled on the price of stocks.

The stock market's rise depended on a continually growing supply of money. But the American money supply was not limitless. After it reached its peak, disaster could occur at any time. Sooner or later, stock prices were bound to fall.

A similar type of financial disaster had occurred a few years earlier. In the years before air conditioning, much of Florida was considered too hot for most people. Therefore, most of Florida's land was undeveloped. But in the 1920s, speculators bought up Florida land and sold it at huge profits. These buyers, in turn, sold it for profit to others. Most people who bought the Florida land had no intention of living there. They only wanted to sell it to someone else and make money. Eventually, there were no more buyers. Those stuck with the land had worthless, undeveloped properties. Many of these buyers went bankrupt.

Many economists saw the country's potential problems. One of them was Herbert Hoover, the United States secretary of commerce. He and other economists tried to advise the new president, Calvin Coolidge. But Coolidge would not listen. "The business of America is business," he proclaimed.[3] "The man who builds a factory builds a temple. The man who works there worships there."[4]

Coolidge reacted to most problems by ignoring them and hoping they would go away. "If you see ten troubles coming down the road, you can be sure that nine will run into the ditch before they reach you," he once said.[5] The nation's economy would turn out to be that tenth trouble.

In 1927, "Silent Cal" issued a brief statement. He chose not to run for president in 1928. A new chief executive would lead the United States. One man seemed the obvious choice.

The Great Engineer

If any man represented the American success story, it was Herbert Clark Hoover. He was the most respected man in Coolidge's cabinet. His influence extended beyond the Commerce Department he headed. Hoover was known as the "Secretary of Commerce and Assistant Secretary of everything else."[6]

Hoover, born in Iowa, was orphaned at age nine. He then went to live with relatives in Oregon. The industrious Hoover worked his way through Stanford University, then became a mining engineer. By the age of forty, he was a millionaire.

During World War I, President Woodrow Wilson called Hoover to direct war relief efforts in Belgium. By most accounts, he did a superb job. After the war, he led relief efforts throughout Europe. The food and medical supplies he delivered saved millions of lives. Wilson's assistant secretary of the Navy admired Hoover's work. "I wish we could make him President of the United States. There could not be a better one," said Franklin D. Roosevelt in 1920.[7]

Hoover was a shy, serious man who lacked personal warmth. Even so, he won the 1928 Republican presidential nomination without difficulty. His opponent, Democrat Al Smith, was an outgoing politician whom Roosevelt dubbed "The Happy Warrior." But voters did not choose their president by personalities in 1928.

Smith came from New York City. Hoover grew up in small towns at a time when most Americans lived in small towns or on farms. Al Smith was a Roman Catholic. Most voters were Protestants, and many held anti-Catholic prejudices. More important, Smith was a Democrat and Hoover a Republican. Hoover's party held power during the prosperous 1920s, and Republicans gladly took credit for the good times. Humorist Will Rogers noted, "You can't lick this prosperity thing."[8] Hoover won by a landslide.

Financiers celebrated Hoover's win. "There has never been a President with a fundamental knowledge of economics better than Mr. Hoover," declared the *Wall Street Journal*.[9] The Wall Street year ended a month later with a joyous confetti celebration. It was the greatest year ever for the stock market. Under Hoover's leadership, 1929 promised to be even better.

Calvin Coolidge (left) and Herbert Hoover (right) served as president during the prosperous 1920s. Their main financial advisor was Albert Mellon (center) who favored tax breaks for wealthy Americans.

1929

Since 1896, investors used the Dow-Jones industrial average to measure the stock market's strength. This number, the average price of leading industrial stocks, reached an all-time high in January 1929. The stock market and the economy looked healthy.

After January, the stock market acted like a roller coaster. Stocks rose, then dropped, then rose again throughout early 1929. The market took a small plunge in March and another in May. Sharp investors saw that the days of continuous growth were over.

Hoover took office in March 1929. "We shall soon . . . be within sight of the day when poverty will be banished from the nation," he predicted during his 1928 acceptance speech.[10] Yet some signs showed otherwise. Many Americans still lived in poverty. The average worker's earnings were only $1,280 per year. Farm incomes, particularly, were less stable than before. Farm prices had dropped 30 percent between 1925 and 1929. Building construction was no longer on the rise. Domestic car sales no longer rose. Everyone who wanted and could afford a car had already bought one. Textile mills and coal mines suffered massive layoffs.

The Federal Reserve Board is an independent government agency which helps oversee the nation's banks. By raising or lowering interest rates to member banks, it can control the supply of available money. In 1929, board members were concerned that more financial trouble lay ahead. They feared that speculators were driving stock prices up beyond the real value of the products companies were producing. People were putting more money than ever into the market. Their money did not go to so-called "safe" stocks like utility companies, which promised small but steady returns. Instead, the speculators gambled on high-profit, high-risk stocks.

The board urged member banks to approve loans for legitimate business deals but not for stock speculation. Then it decided to raise interest rates. Board members hoped this action would curb stock speculation and allow businesses to build their way up to the value of their stocks.

At first, the opposite reaction occurred. RCA stock tumbled almost 10 percent. General Electric fell from $247 to $235 a share. Those losses were short-lived. Americans continued their stock-buying fever, and the market soared during the summer. The stock market was so popular that ocean liners installed brokerage offices. Passengers could buy and sell stocks and watch Wall Street doings from ticker tape machines.

Not everyone shared the stock enthusiasm. Behind the scenes, financier Bernard Baruch sold his stocks and encouraged friends such as Will Rogers to do likewise.

Herbert Hoover, as secretary of commerce, tried to warn Coolidge of a possible economic crisis. But once Hoover assumed office as president, he did virtually nothing. Big businesses were his major campaign supporters, and businesspeople did not want the government tampering with the economy.

Stock Tumble

On September 3, the Dow Jones average reached 381.17. Investors and brokers rejoiced at this new all-time high. Not everyone cheered. Economist Roger Babson predicted, "Sooner or later a crash is coming."[11] Chase Bank president Alfred Wiggin quietly began selling his bank's stock a few days later. On October 16, a committee of the Investment

Bankers' Association reported that speculation "has reached the danger point and many stocks are selling above their values."[12]

The market started slipping on Monday, October 21. Without warning came an onslaught of orders. Brokers received the message: sell, sell, sell. Heavy sales volume caused delays that led to panic. Two days later, 2.6 million shares changed hands. Most transactions involved people selling stock. It was the second busiest trading day ever. Total losses on the stock exchange exceeded $4 billion. This stock tumble convinced many investors that the Wall Street boom was over.

Black Thursday

"I heard it—and I can still hear it—the sound of running feet, the sound of fear," recalled reporter Mathew Josephson.[13] Trading on October 24 started slowly, with few shares changing hands. Then stock prices dived like an out-of-control airplane.

Panicked phone calls took place throughout the nation. These were margin calls, or demands that a stock buyer repay the money he or she had borrowed. Bankers called brokers, seeking the remainder of the margin money they had loaned for stock purchases. Brokers in turn called their customers, trying to get their loans repaid. If the customers could not be reached, the brokers sold their stocks without their permission. Then they used that money to pay off their own debts. Many brokers' customers were small investors who lost all their stocks—and life savings—in one morning.

By noon, a cloud of terror swept the market. Something had to be done to stop the stocks' down-spin. Five of the nation's most important bankers called an emergency meeting. They were Charles Mitchell of National City Bank, Albert Wiggin of Chase Bank, William C. Potter of Guaranty Trust Company, Seward Prosser of Bankers Trust Company, and Thomas Lamont of J.P. Morgan and Company. They met for twenty minutes, then faced the stock exchange members.

"There seems to be some distress selling on the Stock Exchange, so far as we can see," said Lamont. It was a major understatement.[14]

The five bankers took a bold gamble. They pooled money to purchase stocks in major companies. This show of confidence might lure other customers into buying.

Richard Whitney, vice president of the New York Stock Exchange, walked onto the trading floor with the bankers' money. He bought ten thousand shares of U.S. Steel at $205, which was $10 above the market's price. He did the same with other large-company stocks.

The gamble worked. A late-afternoon rally nearly put prices back to the day's starting level. Wealthy investors, who still had money, could buy stocks at low prices. But for hundreds of thousands of amateur investors who lost everything, their stock market game was over for good.

President Hoover and bankers made optimistic statements the following day. The Dow-Jones index rose on Friday. Yet fear rather than hope dominated investors' minds. Many feared what the new week would bring.

On Monday, October 28, prices started plummeting and never stopped. This time, no bankers dipped into emergency funds to halt the selling binge. American Telephone and Telegraph stock lost 34 points and $448 million in value. General Electric plunged 47 points and lost $342.5 million in its value. U.S. Steel dropped 17 points and $142 million.

Shopkeepers and nurses were not the only losers on October 28. Major banks and investment firms reeled from the losses. Weary stock market investors went to bed worried on October 28. The unhappiest day of all awaited them.

"BROTHER, CAN YOU SPARE A DIME?"

Black Tuesday, October 29, was disastrous, but it was not the end of the stock market tumble—the market kept falling. It was November 13 before the market closed with a gain. By that time many stocks were worth only half of the value they had had just two months earlier.

Even during the height of the stock market boom, only 4 million Americans actually invested. But after the October 1929 Crash, the stock market breakdown affected millions of others.

Hundreds of banks had invested huge sums of money in the stock market. Most of that money came from investors' savings. Some banks literally went bankrupt right away. When investors saw a neighbor's bank going out of business, they rushed to withdraw their own savings. These massive withdrawals forced other banks to fold. More than one thousand banks closed in 1930. The Bank of the United States, with fifty-nine branches and more than four hundred thousand investors, was one of them.

Occasionally an investor got lucky. Former Nebraska schoolteacher Inez Warren recalled:

> I got my monthly paycheck on Good Friday. I didn't get to the bank until Saturday, and the cashier asked if I wanted to deposit the check or just take the cash. I said for no particular reason, I would take the cash. I was lucky to have a month's pay in my hands, because the banks closed that Monday.[1]

Thousands of Americans were not as fortunate. Small businesses that had invested their money in the banks were forced to close. When those businesses folded, the employees were out of work. Most larger businesses stayed open, but many laid off workers. They cut production drastically, because fewer people could afford their products.

For some people, the Crash came all at once. Neil Schaffner, owner of a dramatic touring company, recalled July 6, 1930, as his day of doom:

> We ended up our usual big week on the Fourth of July at Ollie, Iowa. We moved down to Fairfield, where we had always had big crowds. On the night of July 6, we played to about $30 gross business. That week, we took in $200 with a show costing us $1,500. We couldn't understand. . . . All of a sudden, the plug was pulled out of the bathtub.[2]

Others saw the Depression hit more gradually. Author Studs Terkel wrote a book, *Hard Times,* which captured people's memories of the Depression. His own memories were vivid. Terkel's mother owned a small hotel in downtown Chicago. Before the stock market crash, the hotel was always full of working people.

Afterward, the hotel was not always full. Fewer and fewer of the guests were working. Many now hung around the lobby most of the day. "The decks of cards were wearing out more quickly. The black and red squares of the checkerboard were becoming indistinguishable," Terkel wrote.[3]

Soup Lines, Bread Lines, and Apple Sellers

Economic downturns had occurred in America every twenty years or so. But nothing matched the severity of the 1930s. During previous depressions, most Americans lived on farms. If nothing else, they could feed themselves. Now, more Americans earned a living from industry than agriculture. The economy was interdependent. If one segment suffered, everyone suffered.

The fortunate people kept their jobs. If they did, their working conditions usually worsened. Most companies lowered their workers' pay. Hourly wages declined 60 percent from 1929 to 1932.

Some no longer paid their workers in cash. Mine companies gave their miners paper called scrip, which they could use in place of money. This paper was good only at expensive company stores. Chicago teachers were also paid in scrip. Banks accepted their scrip, but not at its full value.

At the Depression's height, a quarter of the population was out of a job. The unemployed scrambled for whatever work was available. Ed Paulsen sought a sugar refinery job in San Francisco in 1931. "A thousand men would fight like a pack of Alaskan dogs to get (the job). Only four of us would get through," he recalled.[4]

When joblessness hit, families did all they could to fight the crisis. If there was a savings account, they withdrew it. If there was an insurance policy, it was cashed in. They sold anything they considered a luxury, for whatever price they could get. They borrowed from friends and avoided paying bills.

Men, in particular, took the Depression hard. They held the traditional role of breadwinner. When they no longer brought home money, most felt disgraced and shamed. Some of their neighbors pitied them. Others tried to ignore them.

At first, the unemployed went job-hunting every day. After a while, those searches became less and less frequent. Unemployed people left home, but went to the park instead of looking for work. Their clothes and appearance got dirtier. They did not want to be dirty. Their money was used to buy food for their children instead of soap for themselves.

Some swallowed their pride and begged for change. These were proud people, whose hard work had helped build the nation. The most popular song of the time described one man's plea: "Brother, Can You Spare a Dime?"

That dime, if obtained, could go a long way. "For ten cents you could buy soup greens and you'd get a soup bone," said Chicago resident Carl Lundell. "That would be soup for four people."[5]

During earlier depressions, farmers could at least feed themselves, preserving their crops in fruit jars like these. But by the time of the Great Depression, more Americans worked in industry than on farms, and many lost their jobs.

Charitable groups worked to help the poor. Some started bread lines. In big cities, these lines would extend for several blocks. Soup kitchens opened throughout the nation. Service agencies and private individuals alike served hot meals. Chicago gangster Al Capone operated one of the largest kitchens.

Two out-of-work men kill time in front of a cafe.

In 1930, the International Apple Growers Association sold surplus apples to unemployed men on credit. Suddenly six thousand vendors appeared on New York street corners, selling apples for a nickel apiece. The dreary-looking apple vendor became one of the lasting images of the Depression.

Businesses adjusted to the new American poverty. Even Popsicles changed. The fruit-flavored ice now came in two parts with two sticks. The new Popsicle made it easier for hungry poor kids to share the treat with a brother, sister, or friend.

Despite the hardships, many people kept their good nature. "No one was envious of anyone else, because we were all in the same boat," said Alice Swanson of Chicago.[6]

"Some people were especially kind," remembered Omaha resident Ora Glass. "I had small children, so the milkman said, 'You need this; you've always paid and that's the way it's gonna be.' He went to the company, and it said, 'Fine.' So we always had milk."[7]

Tens of thousands of Americans lost their homes. Often they drifted to makeshift settlements on the outskirts of towns. These settlements always had the same name.

Hooverville

Charles R. Walker wrote in 1932:

I visited the incinerator and public dump at Youngstown, Ohio. Back of the garbage house there are at least three acres of waste land. The place is indeed a shanty town, or rather a collection of shanty hamlets. . . . [It] is called by its inhabitants— Hooverville. . . .

The inhabitants were not, as one might expect, outcasts or "untouchables", or even hoboes in the American sense; they were men without jobs. . . . This pitiable village would be of little significance if it existed only in Youngstown, but nearly every town in the United States has its shanty town for the unemployed, and the same instinct has named them all "Hooverville."[8]

Settlements appeared everywhere. Some of them had enough population to be considered small cities.

Oklahoma City's Hooverville covered approximately one hundred square miles.

There were no rules to Hooverville housing. People lived inside anything that provided shelter. Many of these homes were no larger than doghouses or chicken coops. Rusted out cars provided one type of housing. A house could also be a packing carton, an orange crate, or a piano box. Building materials included whatever could be scrounged from a garbage dump or the street—pieces of wood, tin cans, tar paper, cardboard. The materials were free and not fancy.

President Herbert Hoover was the subject of ridicule. Anything bad about the Depression gained a Hoover nickname. There were "Hoover blankets" (old newspapers which served as cover for homeless sleepers), "Hoover flags" (empty pocket linings turned inside out), "Hoover hogs" (jackrabbits caught for food), and "Hoover wagons" (broken down cars pulled by mules).[9]

"In Hoover We Trusted"

Less than two months after the October 29 crash, President Herbert Hoover addressed Congress. There is no cause for alarm, he said during the State of the Union address. "We have reestablished confidence."[10] Over the next two years, he would issue many such statements. Signs showed that "the nation was turning the corner," he claimed in January 1930. "The worst effects of the crash will have passed in the next sixty days," he stated two months later. In May 1930, Hoover promised, "We have now passed the worst . . . we shall rapidly recover."[11] He missed few opportunities to call the economy "fundamentally sound."[12] On June 30, he declared, "We have now passed the worst."[13]

As more and more people were put out of work, fewer and fewer believed him. Even the Federal Reserve Board cautioned Hoover, "It will take perhaps months before readjustment is accomplished."[14]

Hoover did take actions to ease the financial crisis. Soon after the Crash, he met with business leaders. The president asked them not to cut workers' pay. At first, many went along with the request. But as conditions kept getting worse, most could not keep their promises. Some cut wages. Others laid off employees instead of slashing wages. Others demanded increased production, which meant more work for the same pay from their workers.

Yet Hoover hesitated to use the federal government's powers to halt the economic decline. He felt that state governments, local governments, and private charities should do that work. These groups, however, were strapped for money. They could not take the burden of lifting the nation.

Hoover refused to consider financial relief for individuals. Part of this opposition came from personal beliefs that men and women lost their dignity if the government gave them a handout.

Big businesses also opposed relief. Their money provided the core of Hoover's election support, and he

Debris from junked cars litters a roadside camp.

would not desert them. Millionaire Andrew Mellon served as secretary of the treasury under Hoover's predecessors Harding and Coolidge. Mellon worked mainly to cut taxes for the wealthiest Americans. Hoover had little use for Mellon. But he kept him as treasury secretary anyway, because he feared criticism from the business community if he did otherwise.

That fear of opposition also made him sign the Smoot-Hawley bill in 1930. Economist Paul Douglas gave Hoover a petition with signatures of one hundred economists who opposed the bill. Automobile magnate

Henry Ford called the Smoot-Hawley bill "an economic stupidity."[15] Hoover signed it anyway.

This law created the highest tariff (tax on imported goods) in American history. Republican Congress members who had proposed the bill hoped that high prices of foreign goods would force Americans to buy American-made products. Instead, other countries imposed their own high tariffs. These taxes kept American companies from selling their goods abroad.

Hoover made one important move to free up European money. In 1931, he proposed a one-year moratorium (halt) to debts from World War I. He hoped debtor nations would use that money to buy American consumer goods. Germany instead used the money saved to build up its military forces.

The average American could not identify with the wealthy, aloof Hoover. Most Americans felt he could not identify with them. Even when Hoover tried a humanitarian gesture, it met with protests. When the president appropriated money to the Department of Agriculture for feed for livestock, thousands complained. Why was he willing to feed their animals but not their children?

Hoover's most ambitious program, the Reconstruction Finance Corporation (RFC), gained little popular support. It allowed the president to lend more than $500 million to ailing banks, railroads, and insurance companies.

The RFC ran into problems almost immediately. Central Republic Bank of Chicago received a $90 million loan under the program. Charles G. Dawes, director of the Reconstruction Finance Corporation, was also a director of the bank. Dawes soon resigned from the RFC, and no one accused either Dawes or the bank of wrongdoing. But the incident gave Democrats ammunition in their campaign against Hoover. Here was a president who could not find money to help struggling teachers or unemployed miners, yet he created a program to help rich banker friends.

On July 8, 1932, the stock market bottomed out. The Dow-Jones average, which had reached 452 in September 1929, fell to a sickly 58. U.S. Steel had fallen from $262 to $22 a share. Montgomery Ward had plummeted from $183 to $4. General Motors had dived from $73 to $8.

Critics joked that Hoover's policy of "rugged individualism" was really one of "ragged individualism."[16] Wherever the president went, he found signs that read "In Hoover we trusted—now we are busted."[17] During an appearance in West Virginia, a military guard gave him the traditional twenty-one-gun salute. Someone in the audience muttered, "By gum, they missed him."[18]

Bonus March

Walter L. Waters needed money in 1932. One day that summer, the unemployed World War I veteran had an idea. The government had passed a bill promising war veterans a cash bonus in 1945. Why not give out that bonus now? Waters and neighboring veterans set out from Portland, Oregon, to Washington, D.C., to make his point.

These vets were part of the Allied Expeditionary Force that had helped win the war. Soon news of Waters's "Bonus Expeditionary Force" spread throughout the country. Thousands of men and many of their families joined him in a trip to Washington. By July, some twenty thousand "bonus marchers" and family members descended upon the nation's capital.

Many of the marchers took over abandoned buildings on Pennsylvania Avenue. Most, however, settled across from the Capitol along the Potomac River. The Anacostia Mud Flats, now housing the Bonus Expeditionary Force, became America's largest Hooverville. Pelham Glassford, the District of Columbia chief of police, sympathized with the marchers. He persuaded the Army to loan them tents and cots.

Others were not so sympathetic. Herbert Hoover opposed the immediate bonus. Congress debated the idea. While the House of Representatives and Senate discussed the measure, the bonus marchers waited. They demonstrated for the bill, but the demonstrations were peaceful.

The House passed a bonus bill in July. The Senate, however, turned down the measure. Most marchers, when they heard of the bill's failure, returned home. More than eight thousand six hundred stayed in Washington, D.C. They showed no signs of leaving.

To Hoover, they were an embarrassment. Yet he at first refused to force them from their temporary homes.

Others, including General Douglas MacArthur, saw them as a danger.

Hoover finally listened to MacArthur's advice. He ordered the police to evict the marchers from the abandoned buildings. The police moved on the morning of July 28. Around noon, someone threw a brick at a police officer. The police reacted by firing at innocent marchers. Two hours later, two marchers lay dead.

Later that afternoon, MacArthur led troops down Pennsylvania Avenue. At first some veterans cheered the soldiers. They thought the troops were there to help them. They soon learned otherwise.

Hoover did not order MacArthur to rout the Anacostia squatters. The general did so anyway. His troops scattered the marchers with swords, tear gas, and bayonets. Their horses trampled women and children. Then the soldiers set fire to the campsite. Dwight Eisenhower, who served under MacArthur, called it "a pitiful scene."[19]

Hoover declared, "Thank God we still have a government that knows how to deal with a mob."[20] The veterans who limped home, their wives, children, and friends thought otherwise. The president was no longer an object of ridicule. He was an object of hatred.

Lame Ducks

The Bonus March fiasco sealed an already doomed election.

Republicans nominated Hoover even though his defeat was certain. They would be admitting their

Bonus marchers gathered at the United States Capitol for speeches in the summer of 1932. A few days later, federal troops chased the marchers from Washington, D.C.

failure by not backing their president. And no other Republican wanted to face a humiliating loss.

Hoover lost in November. It was the most one-sided election since 1864. Franklin D. Roosevelt won the election—the same man who had praised Hoover only twelve years earlier.

Republicans lost the presidency, both houses of Congress, and the confidence of the American people. They were truly "lame ducks," defeated politicians waiting until their terms expired.

The economy, however, did not sit idly. Things only got worse in the winter of 1932–1933. By March 1933, about nine thousand banks had failed, wiping out the savings of millions of Americans.

A new bank panic began in February 1933. On February 14, worried investors made massive withdrawals from Detroit banks. Michigan's governor called a "bank holiday"—closing all banks until further notice.

Ten days later, customers made panicked withdrawals from Baltimore banks. This led to a bank holiday in Maryland. Similar actions took place in other states during the next two weeks.

March 4, 1933, was Inauguration Day. Hoover would leave the White House and Roosevelt would enter it. Governors of New York and Illinois called bank holidays at dawn. They feared runs at the major banking centers of New York City and Chicago.

A tired and weary Herbert Hoover rode to the inaugural site. He told an aide, "We are at the end of our string. There is nothing more we can do."[21]

4

FDR

On Inauguration Day, 1933, America faced a national crisis. Thousands of banks had gone out of business, and millions of workers were unemployed. It would take an extraordinary leader to guide the country from economic ruin. America found such a hero, but he was an unlikely one.

Young FDR

If anyone was "born with a silver spoon in his mouth," it was Franklin Delano Roosevelt. His family had wealth. It was not the recently-acquired wealth of capitalists. Instead, it was the wealth of American aristocracy. Young Franklin had twelve ancestors who came to America on the *Mayflower* and others who were among European royalty. Distant relatives included eleven former United States presidents. Neighbors along New York's Hudson River Valley had known and respected the Roosevelts for generations.

Roosevelt's father James and mother Sara rejoiced at the birth of their son in 1882. Franklin Roosevelt grew up happy, safe, and more than a little spoiled. By the time he was sixteen years old, he had visited Europe eight times.

Franklin attended Harvard, where he was known more for his yachting skills than his grades. At Harvard, he fell in love with the woman who became his wife.

Some people say that opposites attract. That seemed to be the case with Franklin Roosevelt. Young, handsome, wealthy Franklin Roosevelt could have dated many women. His fourth cousin, Eleanor Roosevelt, was a plain, shy orphan. Yet she had qualities that attracted him. He admired her intellectual abilities. She also showed great concern for other, less fortunate people.

Franklin idolized Eleanor's uncle, former president Theodore Roosevelt. When Eleanor and Franklin were married in 1905, Theodore (who was Franklin's fifth cousin) gave the bride away. Franklin was aware of Theodore's career path—New York state assembly, assistant secretary of the Navy, governor of New York, president. He followed a similar one.

Sunrise at Campobello

Roosevelt's state senate district was wealthy and overwhelmingly Republican. Even the most loyal Democrats gave him little chance of winning when he ran in the 1910 election. But Franklin Roosevelt, a Democrat, refused to listen to scoffers. He toured the district in his red car, shook as many hands as possible, and squeezed out a narrow victory.

Franklin supported Woodrow Wilson for president in 1912. The new chief executive rewarded Roosevelt by making him assistant secretary of the Navy. By most accounts, he was a hard-working administrator. But skills in the Cabinet do not always mean election victories. Roosevelt was trounced in a 1914 Senate election. Six years later, he ran for vice president with James M. Cox. Republicans Warren Harding and Calvin Coolidge defeated Cox and Roosevelt. "It wasn't a landslide," noted Joseph Tumulty, President Wilson's private secretary. "It was an earthquake."[1]

Even with the loss, Franklin Roosevelt's future appeared bright. Voters throughout the country now knew him. His possibilities appeared limitless—until one summer day in 1921.

The Roosevelts were vacationing at their summer home at Campobello, New Brunswick, in Canada. It was a typical busy day for the active Franklin Roosevelt. He sailed with his sons, fought a small forest fire, then refreshed himself with a swim in the cold ocean water.

When he woke up the next day, he could not move his legs. Franklin Roosevelt had contracted the polio virus a few weeks earlier. The swim tightened his muscles and put him into shock. Although he tried hard, he never walked unaided again. A few months later he received seven-pound leg braces, which would be his companions for the rest of his life.

Roosevelt refused to feel sorry for himself. His self-confidence allowed him to challenge this physical disability. His wealth permitted him to work full-time on rehabilitation.

In one respect, the ailment helped him in life. Before contracting polio, Roosevelt had seen suffering only from afar. Frances Perkins, his secretary of labor, later commented, "The man emerged . . . with a deeper philosophy. Having been to the depths of trouble, he understood the problems of people in trouble."[2] By 1928, he re-entered the political scene. There were political wars to be fought, and he was one of the fighters.

The Happy Warrior

Politics came naturally to Al Smith. The New York City native, in his trademark brown derby hat, had a smile and a handshake for everyone. He rose through the ranks of Tammany Hall, New York's political organization to become the state's governor. Along the way he gained an ally—Franklin Delano Roosevelt.

Even after the polio attack, Roosevelt managed to help his friend. He aided in Smith's 1922 re-election campaign. Two years later, Smith sought the Democratic nomination for president. Franklin gave the nominating speech. He also gave Smith a nickname that stuck—"The Happy Warrior."

Four years later, Smith won the nomination. Franklin Delano Roosevelt (or FDR, as he was increasingly known) again placed Smith's name in nomination for the presidency. It proved to be an important speech. Roosevelt, more than most, realized the importance of the new medium of radio. He intended his speech as much for a nationwide radio audience as for those in the convention hall.

Roosevelt charmed listeners with an excellent radio voice. He also knew how to communicate with that voice. He explained things simply and in a personal manner. Roosevelt peppered his speeches with "my friends" or "you know and I know." When his speeches started, many in the radio audience were mere listeners. When he concluded, they were friends.

This charm helped him in the 1928 race for governor of New York. Republicans swept most of the nation amidst general 1928 prosperity. But the following Inauguration Day, it was Democrat Franklin Delano Roosevelt who was sworn in as governor of New York. He proved to be an energetic leader. Under his leadership, New York provided relief to unemployed residents and reform of the civil service system. Roosevelt won re-election in Depression-torn 1930 by a landslide. At the 1932 Democratic convention, there was little doubt who was the favorite.

"All You Have to Do Is Stay Alive"

Franklin Roosevelt had backed Al Smith for president in 1924 and 1928. In 1932, Smith refused to return the favor. Incumbent Herbert Hoover appeared weak. The now-wealthy Smith wanted the prize for himself.

Southerners wanted one of their own in the White House. Their choice was crusty Texan John Nance Garner, speaker of the House of Representatives. Roosevelt, Smith, and Garner staged a bitter three-way fight for the Democratic nomination.

Franklin D. Roosevelt (wearing wristwatch) campaigns among farmers in North Dakota. Roosevelt won in traditionally Republican farm states in each of his elections.

Delegates cast their votes, and Roosevelt received about half of them. This total ran far short of the two thirds needed for nomination. The second and third ballots showed little gain. Finally, Roosevelt made a deal with Garner. If the Garner delegates backed Roosevelt, he would choose the Texan as his vice-presidential running mate.

Roosevelt secured the nomination on the fourth ballot. During the acceptance speech, he said, "I pledge you, I pledge myself, to a new deal for the American people."[3] The "New Deal" would become the slogan of his administration.

1932 Presidential Election

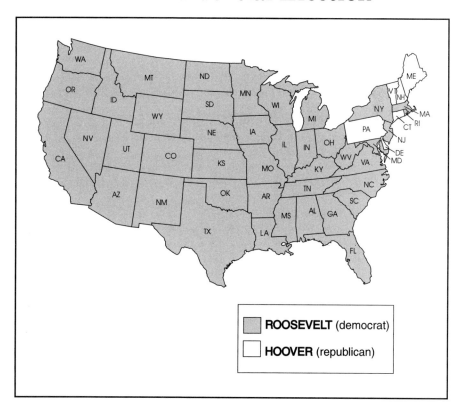

Franklin D. Roosevelt scored an incredible victory in the 1932 presidential election. Herbert Hoover beat the Democrat in only six eastern states—Maine, New Hampshire, Vermont, Connecticut, Pennsylvania, and Delaware.

Few things in life appeared more certain than Hoover's defeat in 1932. According to one joke, Hoover asked Secretary of the Treasury Andrew Mellon for a nickel so he could treat a friend to a soda. "Here's a dime," said Mellon. "Treat them all."[4] After the nomination, California senator William McAdoo told Roosevelt, "Now all you have to do is stay alive until the election."[5]

Garner, too, was convinced the election was a sure thing. He made only one speech—over the radio—during the campaign. Roosevelt, however, travelled and spoke anywhere and everywhere. He wanted to show that his polio was not a work-threatening disability. Roosevelt also wanted the good will of the American people. As president, he would introduce measures that might be unpopular. He could use that good will later.

"Landslide" barely described the Roosevelt victory. The Democrat won by 7 million votes and carried forty-two of forty-eight states. After the election, defeated candidate Hoover tried to work with the victor. Roosevelt refused. He wanted a clean start in his new administration. That meant no association with Hoover's failures.

Roosevelt almost did not live to see the inauguration. On February 15, he was speaking in Miami. An anarchist named Guiseppi Zangara shot at the president-elect. The bullet missed him but hit Chicago mayor Anton Cermak. The mayor, who died a few days later, told the soon-to-be president, "I am glad it was me instead of you."[6]

"TRY SOMETHING"

In 1933, no one knew what to do about the Depression. But everyone saw a need for action. During his campaign, Franklin D. Roosevelt had said, "The country needs . . . bold, persistent experimentation. It is common sense to take a method and try it: If it fails, admit it frankly and try another. But above all, try something."[1] During the next four years, Roosevelt would try and try and try again.

The First Hundred Days

From the beginning, Roosevelt showed his strength. "I shall ask the Congress for . . . broad executive power to wage a war against the emergency, as great as the power that would be given to me if we were invaded by a foreign foe," he said in his March 4 inaugural address.[2] It was now a war against the Depression, and Roosevelt was commander-in-chief.

He showed determination. "The only thing we have to fear is fear itself," he commented, "nameless, unreasoning, unjustified terror which paralyzes needed efforts to convert retreat into advance."[3]

This war began on the banking front. Roosevelt quickly announced a holiday for all American banks. They would be reorganized, he promised. The most stable banks would reopen right away. Others would open a little later. But he did not promise that all banks would reopen.

The next day, a Sunday, the new president called Congress into an emergency session. He called for an end to the export of gold. The precious metal, which was used to assure the value of a nation's currency, could now only be sold to the government. Roosevelt sought a law limiting the power of banks to invest in the stock market. He also moved to cut government expenses.

Congress enacted his proposals a few days later. There was little debate. Most of the members, like Roosevelt, were Democrats. Few wanted to pick a fight with a popular chief executive. Most of all, they were desperate to end the Depression. They would follow any plan that looked good.

On Sunday, March 12, Franklin Roosevelt delivered his first "fireside chat." More than one third of the nation's radios were tuned to this address. Slowly and clearly, he explained the nation's bank crisis. He told listeners what banks did with their money and why the government ordered their closure.

"No solid bank is a dollar worse than when it closed down last week," he claimed. "I can assure you, my friends, that it would be safer to keep your money in a reopened bank than it is to keep it under the mattress." He concluded, "Together, we cannot fail."[4]

Roosevelt stated that the Federal Reserve would transfer currency to reopened banks. Any depositor who wanted money from the bank could get it. But Roosevelt's confidence spread. When banks reopened a few days later, there were more deposits than withdrawals. Roosevelt soon created the Federal Deposit Insurance Commission (FDIC), which insured money in all member banks.

Bank changes were only the beginning of the government's revolution. Roosevelt took the dollar off the gold standard. For years, the government could only mint as much money as it had gold in reserve. By dropping the gold standard, the government could print more money. Since there was now more money than gold, the dollars themselves were worth less. But the increased number of dollars helped business. With more money available, businesses could pay their workers, and the workers could spend more money.

Farmers saw benefits. Roosevelt created a new agency, the Agricultural Adjustment Administration (AAA). It paid farmers to reduce production of staple crops such as corn, cotton, wheat, and tobacco. This way, the remaining crops could fetch higher prices.

One program tackled a particularly hard-hit area. The Tennessee River Valley covered much of the Southeast. Many of the homes lacked electricity. Unemployment ran high. A bill passed in early 1933 created the Tennessee Valley Authority. This agency built a dam in Muscle Shoals, Alabama. Other dams would follow. These dams created electric power, which the government sold at low prices. Available, cheap electricity revolutionized homes and helped businesses.

Unemployed young men got a boost. The Civilian Conservation Corps (CCC) employed a quarter million of them. These youths planted 200 million trees, fought forest fires, cleared beaches, dug drainage ditches, and built reservoirs.

No one claimed the conditions were ideal. Each CCC worker was paid only thirty dollars a month, and most of that money was sent directly to their parents. Discipline was more like boot camp than summer camp. Ray Cordwell helped build a road in Scottsbluff, Nebraska. "When I got up, it was so dark you couldn't see," he recalled. "When we got done, it was so dark you couldn't see."[5]

Their work was worth the effort. George Swanson planted soil erosion dams in Iowa. "The effects wouldn't show for twenty years," he said. "The before and after pictures are amazing. Before, the land was sparse. Now it's beautiful."[6]

For adults who could not find work, Roosevelt created the Federal Emergency Relief Administration. This agency loaned state and local governments money to distribute to needy people.

Roosevelt called for legalization of beer in states that favored it. Fourteen years earlier, the government had outlawed the sale of alcohol. Prohibition, as the ban was known, was a dismal failure. Even though liquor was outlawed, people continued to drink it. Now if people decided to drink, the government could at least levy taxes on alcoholic beverages.

During the Roosevelt administration's first hundred days, a tidal wave of change swept the United States. No American was unaffected by the government's changes. Since then, every president has been evaluated by his accomplishments during his first hundred days in office. None of their accomplishments have come close to those of Franklin D. Roosevelt.

Alphabet Soup

The first hundred days did not mark the end of New Deal energy. Government agencies popped up like mushrooms after a spring rain. Most were known by

Unemployed men wait for relief checks in a small Southern town.

their initials—CWA, WPA, PWA, FSA, SEC. There were so many programs with initials that some people referred to the government as "alphabet soup."

Roosevelt's first relief program, the Federal Emergency Relief Administration (FERA), failed to meet the needs of the poor. Besides, a direct dole to the poor was not what the Roosevelt administration wanted. Thus the Civil Works Administration (CWA) was created to help the jobless through the winter of 1933–1934.

At its peak, the agency employed 4 million men and women. For some, the CWA provided the first paycheck they had seen in years. Hank Oettinger grew up in Wisconsin. He said:

> I can remember the first week of the CWA checks. It was on a Friday. . . . Everybody was out celebrating. It was like a festival in some old European city. . . . They had the whole family out. . . . If Roosevelt had run for President the next day, he'd have gone in by a hundred percent.[7]

The Public Works Administration (PWA) financed the creation of public buildings and more. It was responsible for 10 percent of all new transportation facilities in the country at the time and 15 percent of new hospitals. The PWA built 65 percent of all city halls and courthouses, and 70 percent of all educational buildings.

What did the PWA create? Almost anything. The Triborough Bridge in New York City was a PWA project. So was Boulder (now Hoover) Dam in Nevada, a swimming pool in Wheeling, West Virginia, the zoo in

Lane Technical High School on Chicago's North Side was one of the many public buildings constructed through New Deal programs.

Washington, D.C., a mental hospital in Caramillo, California, and the Lincoln Tunnel connecting New York City and New Jersey.

A new agency began providing work in 1935. The Works Progress Administration (WPA) started with the largest peacetime expenditure in American history—$4.8 billion. Any work was better than none, said WPA director Harry Hopkins. "Give a man a . . . [handout] and you save his body and destroy his spirit. Give him a job and you save both body and spirit," he claimed.[8]

Nobody got rich doing WPA work. There was not enough money to pay large salaries to the army of WPA workers. Besides, the government did not want to discourage workers from seeking jobs with private businesses.

Critics charged that some WPA jobs were make-work efforts that served no real purpose. Some jobs seemed out-and-out silly. The WPA paid a Californian named John Steinbeck to take a census of dogs on the Monterey peninsula.

Yet these jobs provided employment. They also meant work for other people. Fourteen-year-old Marjorie Blakemore made sweet potato, apple, and apricot pies for Chicago WPA workers. "They made $27.50 every two weeks," she remembered. "I sold pies on credit until payday. They always paid."[9]

WPA projects also contributed to America's cultural life. Private funding to the arts all but disappeared during the Depression. The WPA made the government a patron of artists, writers, musicians, and actors. Not all work was of the highest quality, but it gave these artists a creative outlet as well as a paycheck.

Post offices, schools, and other Depression-era buildings received the fruits of the WPA's Federal Artists Project. Colorful murals adorned many of these buildings. Some of the murals had fanciful or abstract themes. Others celebrated history. Many showed an idealized version of Depression life.

The Writers' Project helped document America. Writers from each state produced books which detailed the state's history, attractions, and culture. Other projects preserved priceless records of the country's

This mural showing American resources is one of many at Lane Technical High School. Thousands of Works Progress Administration (WPA) murals graced schools, post offices, and other public buildings.

history. One project gathered the reminiscences of two thousand former slaves.

Even if the WPA itself produced no literary classics, it played a major role in literature. Writers, assured of a steady check, could concentrate on other work. Richard Wright wrote his masterpiece *Native Son* while also doing Writers' Project work. The Writers' Project also employed future literary giants such as Ralph Ellison, John Cheever, and Saul Bellow.

WPA artists worked on a variety of projects, including painting the cover of this historical community pamphlet.

Musicians also benefited from the WPA. Government-created orchestras played throughout the nation.

The Theater Project proved the most controversial of the artistic groups. Troupers such as Orson Welles, Joseph Cotten, John Huston, Arlene Francis, and Burt Lancaster performed in popular and classic plays. In 1935, three hundred fifty thousand people saw Theater Project productions each week. Some acting groups also presented "living newspapers" which commented on current events. Some commentaries angered many people. Pressure from Congress members forced the WPA to drop the Theater Project in 1939.

The Farm Security Administration (FSA) oversaw rural affairs. It recorded American life in a series of superb photographs. This was not a make-work project. Instead, top-notch photographers created valuable records of life in the 1930s. Project director Roy Stryker had a keen sense of history. He made sure that photographers included "the kinds of things that a scholar a hundred years from now is going to wonder about. A butter churn. A horse trough. Crank-handle telephones. . . . The horse and buggy. The milk pails and the cream separators. . . . Symbols of the time."[10]

The Works Progress Administration (WPA) hired actors such as these to perform around the country.

Stryker insisted that his photographers know about their subjects. Once a photographer was asked to shoot a story on cotton. He confessed to Stryker that he knew little about the plant. Stryker said:

> We sat down and we talked almost all day about cotton. We talked well into the night. I told him about cotton as an agricultural product, cotton as a commercial product, the history of cotton in the South, what cotton did to the history of the country, and how it affected areas outside the country. By the time we were through, [he] was ready to go off and photograph cotton.[11]

Roosevelt sought to prevent a repeat of earlier stock market disasters. The 1934 Securities Exchange Act created the Securities and Exchange Commission (SEC). This agency acted as a watchdog to protect investors. It required anyone offering stocks to file a statement of financial information about the stock being sold.

One major New Deal program was never referred to by its initials. Social Security provided an old age pension for persons over age sixty-five and unemployment compensation for those out of work. Other poor people—blind and disabled people as well as dependent children—also were eligible.

Social Security money came from a tax on workers and employers. It was not a perfect plan. Many categories of workers (farmers, for example) were not eligible. Payroll deductions cut purchasing power. Since rich and poor people were taxed at the same rate, it indirectly penalized poor people. Some states, to recover money that was now going to the federal government, created sales taxes. These, too, were taxes that hurt the poor more than the rich. Despite its problems, Social Security quickly became an accepted part of American life.

NRA

Bands played, hundreds marched, and thousands watched along downtown New York City in 1933. The government sponsored this parade to rally Americans for the key program of the New Deal.

Roosevelt realized that all of the programs in the alphabet would not save the economy if the private economy did not improve. At the same time, an unregulated economy was not the answer. Cutthroat competition only made certain businesses richer while bankrupting many others. Something had to be done for the economic health of businesses and workers.

He proposed, and Congress passed, the National Industrial Recovery Act. This act created the National Recovery Administration (NRA), which sought cooperation among industries. Under the NRA, management and labor councils from each industry would agree to "codes of fair competition." These codes set maximum working hours and minimum wages within the industry. Section 7A of the NRA permitted workers to bargain collectively through unions.

The government could not enforce the NRA. But the Justice Department could prosecute signers who later violated the codes. Mainly, it relied on public pressure for cooperation. Businesses that cooperated were allowed to post the NRA blue eagle emblem and use it in advertisements. "We do our part," the emblem declared.

Americans at first rallied behind the plan. More than five hundred industries signed codes by midsummer, 1933. These industries included more than 21 million workers. Textile workers, shipbuilders, and even graveyard workers had their own codes.

Roosevelt signed the NRA into law on June 16. A fireside chat on October 22 declared its success. The president claimed the law put an end to child labor and long-hour sweatshops. NRA director Hugh Johnson claimed that 96 percent of commerce and industry were in compliance with the act.[12]

Other observers saw different results. *Harper's* reporter George Leighton toured four Eastern states in the autumn of 1933. He found that companies openly or secretly violated the codes. NRA compliance boards often consisted of members with close ties to the area's leading employers. Often they were afraid to criticize violators.

Critics attacked even a minimal regulation of business. Publisher William Randolph Hearst said NRA stood for "No Recovery Allowed." Some African Americans did not feel they were getting benefits from the program. They claimed NRA meant "Negroes Ruined Again."[13]

At first, the NRA was meant to last only two years. Roosevelt fought successfully for its renewal. His joy

SEC. 7

(B) THE PRESIDENT SHALL, SO FAR AS PRACTICABLE, AFFORD EVERY OPPORTUNITY TO EMPLOYERS AND EMPLOYEES IN ANY TRADE OR INDUSTRY OR SUBDIVISION THEREOF WITH RESPECT TO WHICH THE CONDITIONS REFERRED IN CLAUSES (1) AND (2) OF SUBSECTION (A) PREVAIL, TO ESTABLISH BY MUTUAL AGREEMENT, THE STANDARDS AS TO THE MAXIMUM NUMBER OF HOURS, MINIMUM RATES OF PAY, AND SUCH OTHER CONDITIONS OF EMPLOYMENT AS MAY BE NECESSARY IN SUCH TRADE OR INDUSTRY OR SUBDIVISION THEREOF TO EFFECTUATE THE POLICY OF THIS TITLE; AND THE STANDARDS ESTABLISHED IN SUCH ARGUMENTS, WHEN APPROVED BY THE PRESIDENT, SHALL HAVE THE SAME EFFECT AS A CODE OF FAIR COMPETITION.

(C) WHERE NO SUCH MUTUAL AGREEMENT HAS BEEN APPROVED BY THE PRESIDENT, HE MAY INVESTIGATE THE LABOR PRACTICES, POLICIES, WAGES, HOURS OF LABOR, AND CONDITIONS OF EMPLOYMENT IN SUCH TRADE OR INDUSTRY OR SUBDIVISION THEREOF; AND UPON THE BASIS OF SUCH INVESTIGATION, AND AFTER SUCH HEARINGS AS THE PRESIDENT FINDS ADVISABLE, HE IS AUTHORIZED TO PRESCRIBE A LIMITED CODE OF FAIR COMPETITION FIXING SUCH MAXIMUM HOURS OF LABOR, MINIMUM RATES OF PAY, AND OTHER CONDITIONS OF EMPLOYMENT IN THE TRADE OR INDUSTRY OR SUBDIVISION THEREOF INVESTIGATED AS HE FINDS TO BE NECESSARY TO EFFECTUATE THE POLICY OF THIS TITLE . . .

Section 7 of the National Recovery Act allowed the president to establish limited codes of competition for various industries. The NRA was declared unconstitutional by the United States Supreme Court in 1935.

was short-lived. The Supreme Court declared the NRA unconstitutional on May 27, 1935.

The administration salvaged part of the NRA. New York Senator Robert Wagner sponsored a bill to protect unions and those who joined them. This bill replaced a section of the now-deceased NRA. It created the National Labor Relations Board (NLRB). This board could stop unfair practices by employers who sought to block union formation. Workers could bargain collectively and choose whom they wanted to represent them.

Dear Mr. (or Mrs.) Roosevelt

To millions of Americans, Franklin D. Roosevelt was more than just their president. They saw him as their friend, an honorary, and honored member of their family. No court decisions or newspaper editorials could shake their faith.

"Every house I visited had a picture of the President," noted a South Carolina social worker.[14] The picture might be a color print or a faded newspaper clipping. But it stood on the family's mantle or another place of honor.

Eleanor Roosevelt also earned her share of that praise. Unlike previous first ladies who stayed in the background, Mrs. Roosevelt travelled throughout the country and wrote her own newspaper column. She, like her husband, was a friend to millions.

Adoration for the Roosevelts showed in the letters they received. More than four hundred fifty thousand

First Lady Eleanor Roosevelt's popularity matched that of her husband, Franklin. She travelled the nation promoting programs for underprivileged people.

letters reached the White House in the week following inauguration. For years, they received five to eight thousand letters weekly.

President and Mrs. Roosevelt did not read each letter personally. But aides showed them a sample of the mail. Louis Howe later commented, "a personal letter from a farmer or a miner or little shopkeeper or clerk who honestly expresses his conviction, is the most perfect index to the state of the public mind."[15]

More women than men wrote. Men most often sought money or work, and they wrote to Franklin Roosevelt. Requests for clothing came from women. They wrote to Eleanor.

Conservative Roosevelt opponents also wrote to the president. They blamed their problems on poor people and opposed any redistribution of wealth. Rebellious souls of all varieties vented their complaints.

But many letters were admiring or even adoring. The writers compared the president and first lady to saints or religious leaders. The Roosevelts were perceived as parents of America or personal friends. There were problems in the country, letter writers admitted. But those problems were caused by bureaucrats in the administration, not the first family.

Only Maine and Vermont

Democrats swept the nation in the 1934 elections. *The New York Times* called it "the most overwhelming victory in the history of American politics."[16] Republican election winners of any kind were rare indeed.

Alfred Mossman Landon was one of those victors. Landon, a successful independent oil producer, won re-election as governor of Kansas. He was the only Republican governor west of the Mississippi River. Since many Americans blamed the Depression on "Eastern economic interests," Republicans sought a 1936 presidential candidate from another region of the country. The likable Landon was an obvious choice.

Landon hardly fit the mold of a traditional Republican. He had supported former Republican president Theodore Roosevelt's Bull Moose Party, not the more conservative Republicans, in 1912. He had voted against Republican nominee Calvin Coolidge in 1924. He supported Social Security and other New Deal measures.

Roosevelt and Landon got along well. Even so, the campaign was bitter. Switchboard operators at the conservative *Chicago Tribune* answered phones by saying, "There are only __ more days to save the American way of life."[17]

Democrats charged that Republicans did not care about the common people. "Governments can err: Presidents do make mistakes," Roosevelt said. "But better the occasional faults of a Government that lives in a spirit of charity than consistent omissions of a Government frozen in the ice of its own indifference."[18]

Class differences more than any other factor determined voting patterns. Win Stracke sang in the choir of Chicago's affluent Fourth Presbyterian Church. "I looked out over the congregation . . . and it was one sea of yellow," he recalled. "Everybody was decorated with large yellow Landon sunflower buttons. [It] suddenly made me realize there is such a thing as class distinction in America."[19]

Literary Digest, a respected magazine, conducted polls before every presidential election. They employed the same method they had used in previous elections—polling by telephone calls. The magazine failed to consider that many impoverished Americans could not afford telephones.

The magazine predicted a Landon landslide—320 electoral votes for Landon to 161 for FDR. Young pollster George Gallup came up with a different result—477 electoral votes for Roosevelt, 42 for Landon, and two states undecided. Roosevelt's campaign manager, James Farley, made a prediction that sounded outrageous. He declared that his candidate would carry every state except Maine and Vermont.

On election night, Farley had the last laugh. Roosevelt got nearly 28 million votes, while Landon took just under 17 million. Six million more Americans voted in 1936 than four years earlier. Of those 6 million, 5 million went with the Democrat. Landon carried Maine and Vermont, as Farley predicted. Roosevelt won the other forty-six states.

About 80 percent of union members, unskilled workers, and people on relief voted for Roosevelt. He even carried about 42 percent of upper-income voters. Roosevelt led the greatest landslide in presidential election history. Other Democrats came into office with him. Roosevelt's party had more than a three-quarters majority in both the Senate and the House.

Roosevelt now had the executive and legislative branches of government firmly in his control. It appeared he could do anything he wanted.

Depression took on many forms in America's heartland. Some were natural, while others were manmade. Massive dust storms blew away the land, and economic misfortunes blew away people who had tilled that land for decades.

DUST BOWL

Storms and Foreclosures

The first great storm hit South Dakota on November 11, 1933. Suddenly a huge black cloud turned the midday sky darker than midnight. The storm blew all afternoon and well into the night. No one dared travel outside without covering his or her face with a handkerchief. The storm blew through Chicago the next day and travelled as far east as Albany, New York.

It was no isolated incident. Dozens of storms sent dirt and sand flying through the Great Plains. Kansas resident Eleanor Williams recalled, "If a roller came from the north we could recognize the rich black topsoil from Nebraska and Colorado. If it came from the south, we'd get the red dust of Oklahoma. Our topsoil would be exchanged in a day or so as it blew away to a neighboring state."[1] Violent winds sometimes exceeded seventy miles per hour. "A newly painted bus

A family rushes to the safety of their plains home during a dust storm of the 1930s.

would find the paint stripped away instantly by blowing sand," recalled Nebraskan Ray Cordwell.[2]

The storms choked people, suffocated animals, and often kept visibility near zero. "You'd be driving in Kansas and you couldn't see the front of your car," Cordwell said.[3]

Such storms became so common that the Great Plains area became known as the "Dust Bowl." One cause of the Dust Bowl was natural. The Great Plains went through a period of drought in the 1930s. These dry periods were not unusual. Since 1889, the Great Plains averaged one drought year in every six.

This time, however, conditions were different. Generations of overgrazing had destroyed much of the region's grass. This grass had held much of the topsoil in place. Homesteaders had plowed up other lands. These lands, too, went flying during the storms.

Nature, along with financial conditions, spelled economic ruin for thousands of farmers. Even in the best of times, many barely survived. They borrowed in the spring to buy seed and supplies. When the harvests came, they paid back their loans. If the harvest was bad, they remained in debt.

Farmers had little control over the prices they received. Their production usually exceeded demand, so prices remained low. Occasionally farmers tried to keep their products off the market. They hoped to create a scarcity, which would drive up prices. They argued and sometimes fought with other farmers who felt they needed to sell their goods, no matter what the price.

Mike Reno of western Iowa started the Farm Holiday Association. This group took militant action in 1930 to prevent farmers from reaching markets in Sioux City, Iowa. Farm Holiday Association members stopped farmers' trucks and dumped their milk. Some farmers needed escorts from deputy sheriffs to get to Sioux City. Eventually, the Association members and farm producers reached a truce.

When farmers could not pay their debts, banks foreclosed on their mortgages and took over the farms. Banks tried to sell off the property of debt-ridden farmers. Sometimes their attempts were less than successful. Neighbors often united to buy the auctioned goods for minimal prices. A prize horse might go for only a quarter, a cow for a dime. Afterward, the buyers would return the goods to the farmer. Outsiders tried to grab a bargain at these auctions. Neighbors let these exploiters know—in a friendly way or otherwise—that they were not welcome.

A farmer who lost title to his or her land might still stay on it by becoming a tenant farmer, paying rent to the new owner. Or the farmer could become a sharecropper, working the land for a percentage of the crops. Even those choices might be short-lived.

Sharecroppers pick cotton on a farm in Mississippi.

Bank foreclosures of small farms led to fewer but bigger farms. Wealthier farm owners could afford to buy the latest machinery. One man working a tractor for about a dollar a day could do the work of several farm families. These families might have been on the land for decades. But they were no longer needed to raise crops. They had to go. Many families moved to town and went on relief. Others hit the road.

"I've Been Doin' Some Hard Travellin'"

Unemployed Americans sought work near their homes. All too often, there was no work to find. Many left to find a new job—wherever that might be. Hundreds of thousands of Americans went by boxcar, by auto, or by thumb, searching for work.

The Missouri Pacific railroad kept records of freight car migrants. The railroad counted 13,475 migrants in 1929. Two years later, it counted 186,028 on its railroad alone. Some of the boxcars were so crowded, they had standing room only.

Railroads hired special police to evict the illegal travellers. If caught, they might be put to work repairing tracks. When the numbers of riders became too great, many police gave up their futile effort. In some cases, railroad conductors ordered extra boxcars to accommodate the migrants.

Men comprised most of the boxcar riders. Women, however, also rode the rails. Many disguised themselves as men, to ward off sexual advances. Boys and

During times of economic stress, hitchhiking became a common means of travel.

even girls joined the cross-country migrations. Often they left home to ease their family's financial burden.

"When a train would stop in a small town and the bums got off, the population tripled," recalled former rider Frank Czerwonka.[4] Some went to the local "Sally"—Salvation Army outpost. Most stopped at hobo jungles, settlements outside of town. They grabbed food and shelter while learning of possible work opportunities.

Many went to local residents' houses. They sought a job or a meal or both. If someone gave them a handout, they left marks near the house. These signals told

After riding the rails, two men stop in town.

future visitors of the homeowner's generosity. One mark might mean that a home would provide a meal. Another meant that the homeowner expected work for food. A different mark meant that the visitor could sleep in the family's barn.

By the mid-1930s, a different group of migrants appeared. These were the tenant farmers who were forced off their land. Many came from the Southwest. They were known as "Okies"—those from Oklahoma— or "Arkies"—from Arkansas.

Thousands flocked to California. There, they heard, people could find steady work. They crammed

Evicted sharecroppers huddle near their possessions along on U.S. Highway 66.

their old cars with family members, dogs, and any possessions that would fit. Then they set out on the perilous journey through the southwestern desert.

California hardly extended a welcome to its would-be residents. Many were greeted by the "hobo express" or the "bum blockade." In some towns, migrants were thrown onto a truck (the "hobo express"), driven to the edge of town, and warned not to return. Sometimes a local posse met a freight train. Guns in hand, the posse members made sure the travellers remained in their boxcars. Authorities at the California state line (the "bum blockade") stopped migrants before they could enter. When one migrant sued to stop the illegal blockade, he and his family were intimidated by police. He withdrew his lawsuit.[5]

Blockades did not prevent people from streaming into California. An estimated three hundred fifty thousand migrants entered the state in the early 1930s. More than two hundred thousand teenagers slept in Los Angeles flophouses and missions in 1932 alone. Many of them came from different states.

The Federal Emergency Relief Administration provided funds for the care of "resident, transient, or homeless persons." It set up "Uncle Sam hotels" in every state except Vermont. The experiment did not last, however. "It was not popular mainly because migrants are not popular," commented journalist Nels Anderson.[6]

People slept where they could—even occasionally in the local jail. They had to be careful. "In California, I didn't sleep in the jails," said songwriter Woody Guthrie. "I was an Okie fullblood and was afraid I might not get out."[7]

Woody Guthrie

In the Middle Ages, minstrels journeyed from town to town. These roving musicians sang songs that described the latest news or local life. America had such a minstrel in the Depression years. His name was Woody Guthrie.

Woodrow Wilson Guthrie, named after a soon-to-be American president, was born in Oklahoma City in 1912. Even as a young man, the down-and-outs of society fascinated him. He spent endless hours chatting with the cowboys, railroad men, and hoboes he met at the edge of town. He talked at length with oilfield workers and shopkeepers. Formal education never interested him much, but he read nearly every book he could find. Young Woody devoured books on psychology, philosophy, and religion.

He avoided manual labor if possible. Even so, he held a variety of jobs—sign painter, quick-sketch artist, fortune-teller. Then he hit the roads or the rails.

Boxcar hoboes were not just Woody Guthrie's fellow travellers. Men with names like "Dinner Fly" or "Dick the Stabber" were his people. "Pretty soon I found out I had relatives under every railroad bridge between Oklahoma and California," he claimed.[8] When Guthrie wrote, "I've been doin' some hard travellin', I thought you knowed, I've been doin' some hard ramblin', way down the road," he spoke from experience.

His comrades freely told him the stories of their lives—their pasts, their presents, their hopes, disappointments, and fears. He turned those stories into hundreds of songs. Some were spur-of-the-moment tunes, forgotten the next day. Others survived as great works of American music.

Guthrie sang to anyone who would listen. He sang at union rallies, work camps, Hoovervilles, in boxcars, in jails. His songs celebrated the lives of American people. "Pretty Boy Floyd" told of an Oklahoma Robin Hood who robbed banks and gave money to the poor.

"Pastures of Plenty" described the sad life of migrant workers. "Tom Joad," a seventeen-verse ballad, summarized John Steinbeck's *The Grapes of Wrath*. "The people of Oklahoma haven't got two bucks to buy the book, or even thirty-five cents to see the movie, but the song will get back to them," Guthrie said.[9]

The songs were more than entertaining. Woody Guthrie used them to forge a sense of pride. "I hate a song that makes you think that you're not any good. I hate a song that makes you think that you are just born to lose," he said.

> I am out to sing songs that will prove to you that this is your world . . . I am out to sing the songs that make you take pride in yourself and in your work. And the songs I sing are made up for the most part by all sorts of folks just about like you.[10]

The Grapes of Wrath

John Steinbeck, a native Californian, travelled and observed life. He worked as a migrant laborer and he wrote. The result was the most famous book of the Depression and one of the great works of American literature.

The Grapes of Wrath tells the story of the fictional Joad family. They were simple Oklahoma farmers forced off their land. The Joads covered the range of Depression humanity. They included hot-tempered but idealistic Tom, level-headed Ma, cowardly Connie, and fun-loving Al. Joining them was a preacher who was seeking the truth.

One day, they saw a handbill offering jobs picking fruit in California. The twelve-member family, plus the preacher, set off in a weighted-down jalopy for the promised land.

California's reality proved unhappier than the dream. Thousands of other workers also saw the handbills. The surplus of willing laborers meant growers could keep wages low. A day's work barely kept a family from starvation. One by one, the Joad family left. Some died, and others just wandered away.

Steinbeck told the dramatic story of a Depression migrant family. He also gave detailed descriptions of the life they faced—selling treasured possessions at a fraction of their value, bargaining for food at a roadside diner, doing emergency repair work on a car. *The Grapes of Wrath* captured the many experiences the Okies faced—sadness, fear, violence, and even occasional happiness.

The book criticized banks that took farmers' land and big farm interests that treated migrants poorly. Not surprisingly, those groups condemned the book. When producer Darryl F. Zanuck bought movie rights to the book, some believed he bought them so that no movie would ever be made.

Zanuck, however, made the film. It became a classic. He took special precautions. The movie was shot secretly so that those opposed to it could not interfere. If someone asked, the film crew gave the name of a different movie. Zanuck hired extra "stagehands" (actually bodyguards) in case trouble arose.

Zanuck did not use the book's depressing ending in his movie. Instead, he left viewers with an uplifting message. Tom Joad is running from the law. The family is out of work. An uncertain future awaits. Yet Ma knows the Joads and common folk like them will survive. "[They] can't wipe us out," she says. "Can't lick us. We'll go on forever. 'Cause we're the people."[11]

7

"SHARE OUR WEALTH"

In many ways, the Depression years were considered times of discontent. Franklin D. Roosevelt's 1932 landslide did not mean unanimous support for the president. Unhappy souls throughout the political spectrum sought government change. On another front, labor unions fought a series of battles for better working conditions. These forces created tensions throughout the 1930s.

An EPIC Campaign

During the 1930s, political movements emerged that critics claimed were more radical than the New Deal. The most famous of these movements occurred in California in 1934.

Upton Sinclair had gained fame as a crusading writer. His 1906 book *The Jungle* exposed the working conditions of Chicago's stockyards and helped bring about the Pure Food and Drug Act. Sinclair had a socialist philosophy; he felt the government should control the nation's economy. Sinclair ran for various offices as a socialist, but received few votes.

In 1933, he changed his tactics. He decided to run for governor of California as a Democrat. The confident Sinclair even wrote a premature history of his administration: *I, the Governor of California and How I Ended Poverty: A True Story of the Future.*

Sinclair's book became an instant success, selling two hundred twenty-five thousand copies in one year. It detailed Sinclair's End Poverty in California (EPIC) proposal. Sinclair suggested that the state of California take over unused factories and farms. Unemployed workers and farmers would create products. They would be paid in scrip that could be used in other EPIC facilities. Production for use, not for profit, was Sinclair's aim. He was proposing a government-owned system, which would rival and eventually take over private businesses. EPIC was socialism under a different name.

By August 1934, one thousand EPIC clubs had sprung up throughout California. The EPIC symbol, a bumblebee, appeared everywhere. EPIC sponsored rodeos and drama groups. A newspaper, the *Epic News,* was distributed to nearly a million homes. EPIC fever hit the polls on the day of the Democratic primary election. Upton Sinclair drew more votes than any other Democrat in California history, more votes than his eight opponents combined.

Industry leaders were worried before the primary, and they were terrified after it. Sinclair, if elected, could alter California's economic system and put them out of business.

This fear produced one of the most vicious political campaigns in American history. Louis Mayer of MGM Studios (the state Republican chairman), C. C. Teague of Sunkist Oranges, and Harry Chandler of the *Los Angeles Times* met for three days in Los Angeles. They plotted a relentless negative campaign.

All major newspapers came out against Sinclair. They did not print his speeches. Instead, some quoted characters in Sinclair's novels and used those words as the Democrat's.

More than $10 million poured into the anti-Sinclair campaign. Much of this money went to produce propaganda films. One phony interview showed a wild-eyed communist saying he supported Sinclair's plan. Another newsreel pictured a horde of hoboes riding boxcars to California so that they could take over the property of working people.[1] These so-called newsreels were blatant lies, but Mayer insisted they be run in California theaters that showed his movies. Many moviegoers hissed and booed the propaganda.

Sinclair might have had a chance if Franklin Roosevelt supported him, but the president refused to back the controversial candidate. He agreed to meet with Sinclair, but only on the condition that they not discuss California politics. Sinclair left the meeting feeling he had communicated his message. His supporters waited, but the endorsement never came.

National Democrats hoped Sinclair would drop his campaign, although Republican governor Frank Merriam was too conservative for their tastes. Some

1. GOD CREATED THE NATURAL WEALTH OF THE EARTH FOR THE USE OF ALL MEN, NOT OF THE FEW.

2. GOD CREATED MEN TO SEEK THEIR OWN WELFARE, NOT THOSE OF THEIR MASTERS.

3. PRIVATE OWNERSHIP OF TOOLS, A BASIC FREEDOM WHEN TOOLS ARE SIMPLE, BECOMES A BASIS OF ENSLAVEMENT WHEN TOOLS BECOME COMPLEX.

4. AUTOCRACY IN INDUSTRY CANNOT EXIST ALONGSIDE DEMOCRACY IN GOVERNMENT.

5. WHEN SOME MEN LIVE WITHOUT WORKING, OTHER MEN ARE WORKING WITHOUT LIVING.

6. THE EXISTENCE OF LUXURY IN THE PRESENCE OF POVERTY AND DESTITUTION IS CONTRARY TO GOOD MORALS AND SOUND PUBLIC POLICY.

7. THE PRESENT DEPRESSION IS ONE OF ABUNDANCE, NOT OF SCARCITY.

8. THE CAUSE OF THE TROUBLE IS THAT A SMALL CLASS HAS THE WEALTH, WHILE THE REST HAS THE DEBTS.

9. IT IS CONTRARY TO COMMON SENSE THAT MEN SHOULD STARVE BECAUSE THEY HAVE RAISED TOO MUCH FOOD.

10. THE DESTRUCTION OF FOOD OR OTHER WEALTH, OR THE LIMITATION OF PRODUCTION IS ECONOMIC INSANITY.

11. THE REMEDY IS TO GIVE THE WORKERS ACCESS TO THE MEANS OF PRODUCTION, AND LET THEM PRODUCE FOR THEMSELVES, NOT FOR OTHERS.

12. THIS CHANGE CAN BE BROUGHT BY ACTION OF A MAJORITY OF PEOPLE, AND THAT IS THE AMERICAN WAY.

Upton Sinclair based his 1934 campaign for California governor on these twelve principles. Opponents attacked them as a socialist platform. Nonetheless his book, I, the Governor of California and How I Ended Poverty: A True Story of the Future, *sold hundreds of thousands of copies.*

voters of both parties backed moderate third party candidate Raymond Haight, but Democratic leaders struck a deal with Merriam. They would support him if he would declare his election a bipartisan victory and support the New Deal.

Merriam won the election with 49 percent of the vote, to 37 percent for Sinclair and 14 percent for Haight. Even so, Sinclair could proclaim victories. EPIC followers won twenty-seven state legislative seats. They included future United States Senator Sheridan Downey and future governor Culbert Olson. Sinclair summed up his campaign, "We threw an almighty scare into the minds and hearts of the people who were running the state."[2]

The Priest, the Doctor, and the Kingfish

Roosevelt's strongest enemies were not Republican politicians. Instead, they were three diverse personalities: a radio preacher named Charles Coughlin, a retired doctor named Francis Townsend, and a Louisiana Democratic politician named Huey Pierce Long. Each commanded a large following in the early 1930s.

Charles Coughlin, a Catholic priest in suburban Detroit, began reading his sermons over the radio in 1926. Soon stations around the country carried his broadcasts. By 1930, he was attracting a weekly audience of more than 30 million listeners.

At first, Coughlin backed Franklin Delano Roosevelt. Then he opposed the president, claiming Roosevelt's policies only served the rich. Coughlin's

National Union for Social Justice called for a "living national wage" and nationalized banks.

By 1936, Coughlin's popularity had peaked. After a while, anti-Jewish attacks replaced calls for justice in his sermons. By the end of the year, he was off the air.

In early 1934, elderly physician Francis Townsend wrote a letter to a Long Beach, California, newspaper. The letter proposed a 2 percent sales tax. The government would use this money to pay two hundred dollars per month to each citizen over sixty years of age. Each recipient would have to spend the money within thirty days. Townsend reasoned that with this plan, older people would have the money they needed, the economy would benefit from circulating money, and younger people would take jobs that became open when their elders retired. His plan enjoyed wide popularity. By late 1935, more than 3 million followers joined Townsend clubs.

The plan's opponents were as numerous and varied as its supporters. Government economists claimed that the monthly payments would surpass the combined budgets of the federal, state, and local governments. Groups as diverse as the National Association of Manufacturers, the American Federation of Labor, and the Communist party criticized Townsend's idea. Yet Townsend gained at least indirect results. Roosevelt headed off potential presidential opposition from Townsend followers. His Social Security plan, creating a tax to benefit older and disadvantaged Americans, was similar to Townsend's idea.

Roosevelt's most powerful foe lived in Louisiana. Senator Huey Pierce Long was a spellbinding orator. "[He would] go to places where he'd never been before, where they had never heard him. When he finished [speaking], he had 'em," his son Russell recalled.[3]

As governor, Long had worked wonders with his impoverished state. He created better schools, provided free schoolbooks, and built roads while keeping Louisiana's budget in good order. Unlike many Southern white politicians of the time, he refrained from anti-black prejudice. His enemies, however, called him a dictator who ruthlessly squashed those who stood in his way.

He called himself the Kingfish (after a popular radio character) but declared "Every man a king." His "Share Our Wealth" program promised each family at least five thousand dollars per year.[4] Long's ideas drew a great following, particularly in the South. He made no secret of his desire to become president. Roosevelt allies feared he could siphon enough votes from the president to give Republicans a 1936 victory.

Those fears ended on September 8, 1935. A physician named Carl Austin Weiss, Jr., angered at Long's criticism of his father-in-law, shot the Kingfish to death in the Louisiana state capitol.

After Long's death, election threats to Roosevelt from populist groups largely disappeared. The Canadian-born Coughlin was ineligible to become president, and Townsend considered himself too old to be a candidate. Some of the three men's followers fell behind the candidacy of North Dakota Congressman William Lemke, but Lemke gained relatively few votes.

Labor Pains

The New Deal's National Industrial Recovery Act barely lasted two years. But one section of the NRA survived in an altered form that proved vital to the labor movement. Section 7A gave workers the right to organize unions and deal with owners through collective bargaining. Workers and unions praised the section. Owners hated it.

In the early 1930s, industries went to great lengths to stop independent labor unions. Some formed company unions, which gave workers few benefits. Others took more drastic action. Carnegie Steel near Pittsburgh paid informers thirty-five dollars per day to spy on union activities. The Pittsburgh Coal Company kept machine guns at the mines. Chairman of the Board Richard B. Mellon claimed, "You cannot run the mines without them."[5]

Strong union leaders such as John L. Lewis showed that workers could stand up to management. The result was a series of strikes that spread across the country. More than 1.5 million workers walked off their jobs in 1934 alone.

Some strikes resulted in bloodshed. One battle in Minnesota left two workers dead and another sixty-seven injured. Other workers retaliated by killing two members of a so-called "citizens' army" sponsored by the factory. More than one hundred thousand people showed up at the slain workers' funeral.

In 1934, a strike by the Longshoremen's Union rocked the West Coast. Every major Pacific Coast port except Los Angeles closed, because no one would load or unload ships.

San Franciscans expected a peaceful demonstration for the longshoremen on July 5. Many gathered to watch, and some even sold refreshments. Then the shooting started. Workers, spectators, and bystanders fled wildly as police on horseback ran over the crowd and bashed people with nightsticks. The strikers retreated.

A few days later, workers called a general strike. Businesses everywhere shut down. "No street cars were operating," one journalist wrote. "No buses, no taxis, no delivering wagons except milk and bread trucks which were operated with the permission of the general strike committee."[6] The only restaurants open were those kept open to feed the strikers. The general strike resulted in a compromise that brought gains to the longshoremen.

Lewis saw that workers were making gains. He wanted to see them become even stronger. At the 1935 convention of the American Federation of Labor, (A.F.L.) he proposed that the federation enlist workers in mass production industries such as steel, rubber, and automobile manufacturing. The A.F.L., composed mainly of crafts workers, voted down the idea.

A few weeks later, Lewis formed the Committee (later renamed Congress) of Industrial Organizations within the A.F.L. This C.I.O. was more of an activist group than the A.F.L., and the parent organization ousted it in 1936. Lewis's C.I.O. fearlessly challenged the giant industries, including the nation's largest automaker.

Flint, Michigan

Residents of the industrial city of Flint, Michigan, were awaiting the next day's Christmas activities when they heard the news. Second-shift workers at a General Motors plant there refused to leave their posts or let others enter. The Christmas Eve, 1936, sit-down strike would make headlines throughout the country.

At first, Lewis opposed a General Motors strike. But once it began, it received his complete backing. He declared in a speech that if National Guard troops shot at the strikers, they would have to shoot him first.

Plant managers tried to freeze the workers out by shutting off the plant's heat. The workers stood their ground. Realizing that frozen pipes might cause mechanical problems when the plant reopened, the managers turned the heat back on.

Next, police stormed the building. Workers, using whatever they could find as a weapon, beat back the assault. After forty-four days, General Motors executives settled the strike. The United Auto Workers, affiliated with the C.I.O., became recognized as the workers' bargaining agent.

Strikers rejoiced at their victory. One organizer commented, "Those people sang and joked and laughed and cried, deliriously joyful. . . . Victory . . . meant a freedom they had never known before."[7] They were not the only ones with reason to rejoice. After the Flint strike settlement, C.I.O. membership zoomed from eighty-eight thousand to four hundred thousand in only eight months.

Memorial Day Massacre

The Flint sit-down strike sent shock waves throughout American industry. It produced some astounding results. U.S. Steel, the nation's largest manufacturer, had vowed not to deal with the C.I.O. But secret negotiations brought about a March 1, 1937, announcement. The giant steel company recognized the Steel Workers Organizing Committee, an arm of the C.I.O.

Other large steel companies, together known as "little steel," hardly followed the U.S. Steel example. Bethlehem, Republic, National, Inland, and Youngstown Sheets and Tube refused to sign C.I.O. contracts.

Tensions hit their peak at Chicago's Republic Steel plant. On Memorial Day of 1937, workers there tried to demonstrate for better conditions. Police, fed at company expense, refused to allow peaceful picketing. Workers threw rocks and sticks at police, and the officers answered with gunfire. They shot ten dead and wounded a hundred more. Evidence showed that those slain were trying to run from the police, not toward them to attack.

The "Memorial Day Massacre" scared off many would-be organizers. It would be another four years before Ford Motors, Goodyear Tires, and many steel companies would recognize C.I.O. unions.

8

THE SECOND NEW DEAL

A series of floods greeted Roosevelt after he took the oath of office for his second term. The Ohio and other rivers overflowed their banks during January 1937. Pittsburgh, Pennsylvania, found itself under more than ten feet of water. The Ohio River rose eight feet higher than ever before in Cincinnati, Ohio, seven feet in Louisville, Kentucky. Only heroic efforts by local residents kept Cairo, Illinois, from being overrun by the river. The flooded river drowned nine hundred people and drove half a million from their homes. This was a natural disaster of major proportions. It would not be the only disaster Roosevelt would face.

Court Packing

President Franklin D. Roosevelt headed the executive branch of government. Congress, the legislative branch, was solidly Democratic and appeared to be on the president's side. That left only the judicial branch of government, headed by the Supreme Court.

Roosevelt chafed at Supreme Court decisions which had gutted some of his New Deal programs.

The Court had struck down the Agricultural Adjustment Administration and National Recovery Act and declared state minimum wage laws unconstitutional. One critic wrote:

> The Court not merely challenged policies of the New Deal but erected judicial barriers to the reasonable exercise of legislative powers . . . to meet the urgent needs of the twentieth-century community.[1]

The Supreme Court did not reflect the feelings of the voters, who reelected Roosevelt in 1936 by a landslide. FDR did not have the opportunity to name any justices during his first term. All but two had been appointed by Republican presidents. Roosevelt proposed a plan that would prevent the high court from undoing his work.

Former United States Attorney General James C. McReynolds, the most anti-Roosevelt Supreme Court justice, once wrote a suggestion that the president have the power to appoint a new justice for every justice over age seventy who had served at least ten years and refused to retire. Roosevelt's attorney general, Homer Cummings, saw that document. McReynolds's words would return to haunt him.

Without consulting Democratic leaders beforehand, Roosevelt told them his court plan. Under it, the president could appoint a new judge for every federal judge over age seventy who did not retire. This proposal could expand the Supreme Court up to fifteen members, depending on how many resignations occurred. Roosevelt could appoint up to six new justices.

1. PROPOSED BILL

BE IT ENACTED, THAT—

(A) WHEN ANY JUDGE OF A COURT OF THE UNITED STATES, APPOINTED TO HOLD HIS OFFICE DURING GOOD BEHAVIOR, HAS HERETOFORE OR HEREAFTER ATTAINED THE AGE OF SEVENTY YEARS AND HAS HELD A COMMISSION OR COMMISSIONS AS JUDGE OF ANY SUCH COURT OR COURTS AT LEAST TEN YEARS, CONTINUOUSLY OR OTHERWISE, AND WITHIN SIX MONTHS THEREAFTER HAS NEITHER RESIGNED NOR RETIRED, THE PRESIDENT, FOR EACH SUCH JUDGE WHO HAS NOT SO RESIGNED OR RETIRED, SHALL NOMINATE, AND BY AND WITH THE ADVICE AND CONSENT OF THE SENATE, SHALL APPOINT ONE ADDITIONAL JUDGE TO THE COURT TO WHICH THE FORMER IS COMMISSIONED: *PROVIDED*, THAT NO ADDITIONAL JUDGE SHALL BE APPOINTED HEREUNDER IF THE JUDGE WHO IS OF RETIREMENT AGE DIES, RESIGNS, OR RETIRES PRIOR TO THE NOMINATION OF SUCH ADDITIONAL JUDGE.

(B) THE NUMBER OF JUDGES OF ANY COURT SHALL BE PERMANENTLY INCREASED BY THE NUMBER APPOINTED THERETO UNDER THE PROVISION OF SUBSECTION (A) OF THIS SECTION. NO MORE THAN FIFTY JUDGES SHALL BE APPOINTED THEREUNDER NOR SHALL ANY JUDGE TO BE SO APPOINTED IF EACH APPOINTMENT WOULD RESULT IN (1) MORE THAN FIFTEEN MEMBERS OF THE SUPREME COURT OF THE UNITED STATES, (2) MORE THAN TWO ADDITIONAL MEMBERS SO APPOINTED TO A CIRCUIT COURT OF APPEALS, THE COURT OF CLAIMS, THE UNITED STATES COURT OF CUSTOMS AND PATENT APPEALS, OR THE CUSTOMS COURT, OR (3) MORE THAN TWICE THE NUMBER OF JUDGES NOW AUTHORIZED TO BE APPOINTED FOR ANY DISTRICT OR, IN THE CASE OF JUDGES APPOINTED FOR MORE THAN ONE DISTRICT, FOR ANY SUCH GROUP OF DISTRICTS. . . .

(D) AN ADDITIONAL JUDGE SHALL NOT BE APPOINTED UNDER THE PROVISIONS OF THIS SECTION WHEN THE JUDGE WHO IS OF RETIREMENT AGE IS COMMISSIONED TO AN OFFICE AS TO WHICH CONGRESS HAS PROVIDED THAT A VACANCY SHALL NOT BE FILLED.

In 1937, President Roosevelt proposed a bill which would allow him to appoint new judges when aging justices would not retire or resign. The bill came as a result of Supreme Court opposition to New Deal measures. Even many Roosevelt allies opposed his "court packing" plan, and Roosevelt eventually gave up the idea.

These appointees could assure him a Supreme Court majority.

The reaction to his plan might have shocked the president. Not only Republican foes but also Democrats blasted the idea. His enemies disliked Roosevelt anyway, but even some allies felt his proposal tampered with the Constitution. Hatton Sumner, chairman of the House Judiciary Committee, told his colleagues, "Boys, here's where I cash in my chips."[2] The former Roosevelt ally became a solid opponent afterwards.

Roosevelt finally gave up his "court packing" proposal. But the "nine old men" on the high court got his message. Instead of striking down every New Deal proposal, the court suddenly upheld them.

Aging Justice Willis Van Devanter resigned soon after the court packing announcement. Others also followed him. Roosevelt now filled the Supreme Court with his own choices. Three of them—Hugo Black, Felix Frankfurter, and William O. Douglas—would later be considered among the greatest justices in Supreme Court history.

The court packing issue had its effect on Roosevelt. He had won a battle because the Court no longer opposed him. But he still suffered a loss. Opposition from Congress and the public showed that Franklin Delano Roosevelt no longer was invincible.

The Roosevelt Recession

"I see one-third of a nation ill-housed, ill-clad, ill-nourished," President Roosevelt said in his second

ALL I SAID WAS 'GIMME SIX MORE JUSTICES!'

President Roosevelt was surprised at the widespread opposition to his 1937 "court packing" plan. He soon abandoned the idea of adding more justices to the Supreme Court.

inaugural address.[3] Although the economy showed some improvement by early 1937, Roosevelt's view was correct.

By inauguration day, the economy was seeing improvements. This upturn was short-lived. An August recession cost 4 million workers their jobs. Production, sales, and the stock market plummeted for the next seven months. Roosevelt accepted blame for what his critics called the "Roosevelt Recession."

Roosevelt decided government spending was the answer. He would create new federal programs, even if it meant a budget deficit. Three billion additional dollars went to relief, flood control, public works, and housing.

This "Second New Deal" met with less acclaim than the first. The programs were created to solve existing problems, although many were less than successful.

SECOND INAUGURAL ADDRESS

I SEE A GREAT NATION, UPON A GREAT CONTINENT, BLESSED WITH A GREAT WEALTH OF NATURAL RESOURCES. ITS HUNDRED AND THIRTY MILLION PEOPLE ARE AT PEACE WITH THEMSELVES; THEY ARE MAKING THEIR COUNTRY A GOOD NEIGHBOR AMONG THE NATIONS. I SEE A UNITED STATES WHICH CAN DEMONSTRATE THAT UNDER DEMOCRATIC METHODS OF GOVERNMENT, NATIONAL WEALTH CAN BE TRANSLATED INTO A SPREADING VOLUME OF HUMAN COMFORTS HITHERTO UNKNOWN, AND THE LOWEST STANDARD OF LIVING CAN BE RAISED FAR ABOVE THE LEVEL OF MERE SUBSISTENCE.

BUT HERE IS THE CHALLENGE IN OUR DEMOCRACY: IN THIS NATION I SEE TENS OF MILLIONS OF ITS CITIZENS—A SUBSTANTIAL PART OF ITS WHOLE POPULATION—WHO AT THIS VERY MOMENT ARE DENIED THE GREATER PART OF WHAT THE VERY LOWEST STANDARDS OF TODAY CALL THE NECESSITIES OF LIFE.

I SEE MILLIONS OF FAMILIES TRYING TO LIVE ON INCOMES SO MEAGER THAT THE PALL OF DISASTER HANGS OVER THEM DAY BY DAY.

I SEE MILLIONS DENIED EDUCATION, RECREATION, AND THE OPPORTUNITY TO BETTER THEIR LOT AND THE LOT OF THEIR CHILDREN.

I SEE MILLIONS LACKING THE MEANS TO BUY THE PRODUCTS OF FARM AND FACTORY AND BY THEIR POVERTY DENYING WORK AND PRODUCTIVENESS TO MANY MORE MILLIONS.

I SEE ONE-THIRD OF A NATION ILL-HOUSED, ILL-CLAD, ILL-NOURISHED.

IT IS NOT IN DESPAIR THAT I PAINT YOU THAT PICTURE. I PAINT IT FOR YOU IN HOPE—BECAUSE THE NATION, SEEING AND UNDERSTANDING THE INJUSTICE IN IT, PROPOSED TO PAINT IT OUT ... THE TEST OF OUR ABUNDANCE IS NOT WHETHER WE ADD TO THE ABUNDANCE OF THOSE WHO HAVE MUCH, IT IS WHETHER WE PROVIDE ENOUGH FOR THOSE WHO HAVE TOO LITTLE.

Roosevelt's second inaugural address had optimistic notes. But President Roosevelt also commented that much of America lived in poverty. There was still much work to be done.

The Resettlement Administration (RA) sought to help tenant farmers, sharecroppers, and migrant workers. The RA worked to end racial discrimination, which aroused opposition from many Southern politicians.

Roosevelt signed a labor bill in June 1938. This provided a minimum wage of twenty-five cents an hour (eventually rising to forty cents) and a maximum work week of forty-four hours (to be reduced to forty). It also outlawed child labor for those under sixteen years of age.

He called it perhaps the "most far-sighted program for the benefit of workers ever adopted in this or any

In the South, most movie theaters were segregated. African Americans could only sit in a special "colored" section. The RA worked to end such racial discrimination.

other country."[4] Not everyone agreed. Southern business owners, many of whom paid extremely low wages, disliked this forced wage hike. Some labor unions feared the government was taking over their power. Republicans and even conservative Democrats voiced opposition to the second New Deal.

Roosevelt targeted several Democratic congressional foes in the 1938 Democratic primary elections. His attacks backfired. All of his detractors won. Republicans posted gains in the November general elections. They picked up eight Senate seats and eighty-one seats in the House of Representatives. Statehouses saw thirteen new Republican governors. Even with those gains, Democrats still held wide majorities in Congress and among governors.

By 1939, it appeared that the economy was not going to heal itself fast. It would take some outside force to turn America around. That force was coming.

9

"MAIRZY DOATS AND DOAZY DOATS"

Even in the depths of Depression, life was not all gloom and misery. People found ways to enjoy themselves. Sometimes that enjoyment was something grand and epic. Often, it was as simple as a box in the living room.

Meet Me at the Fair

A sea of colored lights greeted people coming to Chicago's lakefront in 1933. The hundred-year-old city was celebrating with the Century of Progress—a gigantic world's fair.

Light from the distant star Arcturus was captured and converted into energy. This became electricity, which started up the fair.

The fair's 16 million visitors saw exhibits celebrating science and industry. They viewed everything from a recreated Mayan temple to the dentures George Washington wore. Baseball celebrated the fair by holding an all-star game in the White Sox's Comiskey Park. The popular game became an annual event.

Italy honored the fair. Dictator Benito Mussolini sent an air armada across the Atlantic Ocean. Chicago

A Chicago monument honors Italo Balbo, who led an air armada to the city for its 1933 Century of Progress fair. The Chicago event, held during the depths of the Depression, nonetheless attracted 16 million visitors.

residents cheered as the planes landed near the fair. There would be no cheers a few years later. In World War II, many of these same airplanes would be attacking American soldiers.

Sports and Games

Americans continued their love of sports. Baseball remained the national pastime. Fans followed the sixteen major league teams, although attendance at many ballparks dropped. The St. Louis Browns in 1935 drew only eighty-nine thousand fans all season—less than what most teams draw for a good weekend series

Camp members gather to watch a baseball game.

today. Thousands of other fans saw Negro League games, with talented African-American players who were barred from the majors only because of their race.

Other sports also drew fan support. College football remained popular, and interest in the young National Football League grew. Boxing matches drew thousands of spectators. Americans cheered during the 1936 Olympic Games when Jesse Owens won four gold medals. Germany's racist dictator, Adolf Hitler, left Berlin's stadium instead of congratulating the African American.

The Depression era featured many outstanding athletes—Jesse Owens, boxer Joe Louis, and baseball stars Babe Ruth, Jimmy Foxx, Dizzy Dean, and Satchel Paige. But one of the most amazing athletes of the 1930s was a woman. Mildred "Babe" Didrikson played in many different sports and starred in all of them. She won gold medals in the javelin and hurdles, and a silver medal in the high jump during the 1932 Olympics. While touring with an all-male baseball team, she set a women's record by throwing a baseball 296 feet. She won fifty amateur and professional golf tournaments, including fifteen in a row. She even tried boxing.

At-home activities also gained popularity. Jigsaw puzzles enjoyed a boom. Before the Depression, only the wealthy played bridge. Afterward, people throughout the nation enjoyed the card game. But a new game captured America's imagination. Monopoly players vied to build hotels on ritzy Boardwalk and Park Place. People with barely a dime to their names could dream of amassing fortunes.

Over the Rainbow

Americans saved their pennies to go to the movies—from the film palaces of New York and Chicago to the tiny Idle Hour Theater in Glenwood, Missouri. Filmgoers bought more than 60 million movie tickets per week in the early 1930s.

These films rarely showed daily Depression life. Instead, patrons bought tickets to journeys away from

Movie theaters, a major source of entertainment during the Depression, were important features of both big cities and small towns.

their worries. They went almost anywhere. Some followed King Kong up New York City's Empire State Building. Others danced to sophisticated musical numbers with elegantly dressed Fred Astaire and Ginger Rogers. Young and old retreated to the wild west with John Wayne in *Stagecoach*. Millions laughed at the zany comedies of the Marx Brothers and W. C. Fields. Filmgoers by the thousands followed Dorothy over the rainbow to visit the Wizard of Oz or raced with the seven dwarfs to save Snow White.

The most elaborate movie of all ended the 1930s. Atlanta author Margaret Mitchell wrote *Gone with the Wind*, an epic tale of the Civil War era. Movie fans waited breathlessly for the film version of the novel. Dashing Clark Gable was the obvious choice for handsome Rhett Butler. Producer David Selznick surprised many when he chose English-born Vivien Leigh to play the strong-willed Scarlett O'Hara. Movie fans adored the film. *Gone with the Wind* won ten Oscars, including a Best Actress award for Vivien Leigh.

Radio's Golden Age

For the most popular entertainment, people stayed home. At night, families listened to the radio in their living rooms. Radio brought news, music, comedy, and sports from around the country. Best of all was the price. Once a family bought the radio set, the entertainment was free.

People could hear music of all types. There was jazz clarinetist Benny Goodman and his vibrant swing music. Southern listeners enjoyed Nashville's Grand Ole Opry country music show. Silly novelty tunes like "Mairzy Doats and Doazy Doats" and "Three Little Fishies" gave millions a well-needed chuckle.

Radio produced stars that Americans considered close friends. One of them was Jack Benny. He was a vain, foolish cheapskate surrounded by a gang of eccentric friends. When a robber pointed a gun at Jack and demanded, "Your money or your life," the comedian paused, then said, "I'm thinking it over."[1]

Performing musicians reached an audience of thousands over the radio.

Listeners identified with the weaknesses of Jack and his pals. They loved them.

Listeners thrilled to the adventures of the Lone Ranger, masked hero of the Old West. Women particularly enjoyed soap operas, tear-inducing tales of liars, cheaters, gossips, marital problems, and characters with amnesia. Children used their secret decoder rings to help Little Orphan Annie escape from a variety of villains.

Radio shows exercised listeners' imaginations. One favorite program featured Fibber McGee and Molly.

Each week McGee opened his closet door, and an avalanche of junk fell out. "You heard the junk fall out of Fibber McGee's closet, but everyone used their imaginations to determine which junk fell," one listener said.[2]

On October 30, 1938, thousands of Americans panicked. "Everybody was terribly frightened. Some of the women almost went crazy," one witness recalled.[3]

What caused this terror? Orson Welles produced a radio program based on the science fiction novel *War of the Worlds*. Those who tuned in from the beginning realized it was only a radio play. But millions of people who joined the show in progress heard a frightening account of alien monsters invading New York. Even though columnist Dorothy Thompson claimed, "Nothing about the broadcast was in the least credible," the Columbia Broadcasting System and Welles issued apologies afterward.[4] Fears of a martian attack proved unfounded. They would be replaced by more realistic terror of foreign enemies.

10

"THE GREAT ARSENAL OF DEMOCRACY"

While America reeled from the Depression in the 1930s, Germany lay in ruins. After being defeated in World War I, the Germans were forced to make reparations (huge payments) to the allied victors. Inflation struck so hard that the nation's currency became nearly worthless. The Germans blamed the reparations for their plight.

One German politician took advantage of the discontent. Adolf Hitler was a hotheaded extremist who tried to overthrow the government in 1923. His efforts landed him in jail for eight months. During this time, he wrote a book titled *Mein Kampf* ("*My Struggle*"). It detailed his plans for extermination of Jews, communists, liberals, and capitalists. The few Americans who read *Mein Kampf* dismissed it as the work of a lunatic. Germans, however, increasingly rallied behind Hitler. Ten years after his failed overthrow attempt, he became chancellor of Germany.

Hitler built up Germany's military forces. In 1936, he sent troops into the Rhineland, a demilitarized area of western Germany. This action violated the Versailles

Treaty, which Germany had signed at the end of World War I. Britain, France, and the United States, the major allied nations who had defeated Germany in World War I, did nothing to stop him.

The German dictator was not alone in his militarism. Benito Mussolini, Italy's dictator, sent troops to take over the African nation of Ethiopia. Ethiopian leader Haile Selaisse pleaded with the League of Nations, an international peacekeeping organization, for help. The League did nothing.

In 1931, Japan invaded the northeastern Chinese province of Manchuria. It set up the state of Manchukuo, a government that most other nations did not consider valid. By 1937, Japan had invaded Nanking and had slaughtered one hundred thousand Chinese. The Allies did not try to stop this aggression.

A grisly civil war engulfed Spain in 1936. Rebel forces backed by Germany and Italy, and led by Francisco Franco, moved to topple the liberal government. Among major nations only the Soviet Union openly supported the liberals. However, volunteers from around the world, including American writer Ernest Hemingway, came to their aid. These international soldiers often were great in idealism, but poor in military skills.

The Germans used Spain as a testing ground for their newest weapons. They ruthlessly destroyed Spanish towns and villages. In 1939, Spain fell to Franco's Fascists.

Britain and France did not fight the conquerors. Instead, the Allies cooperated with them. In 1938, Hitler demanded the Sudetenland, the western section of Czechoslovakia.

Representatives of Britain, France, Italy, and Germany (but not Czechoslovakia) met in Munich, Germany, to discuss the region's fate. When the conference ended, the Germans had gained the province without firing a shot. Hitler falsely claimed that he wanted no more territory. British Prime Minister Neville Chamberlain displayed the Munich Treaty and declared that he had achieved "peace in our time."[1]

In the United States, Franklin Roosevelt saw the world events unfolding. He was burdened by the Depression at home, yet Roosevelt was preparing for what appeared to be inevitable world conflict.

"A Neutral Nation"

Many Americans in the 1930s sought to keep America out of world conflicts. They included aviation hero Charles Lindbergh, labor leader John L. Lewis, and architect Frank Lloyd Wright. Business magnate Joseph Kennedy, father of a future Democratic president, opposed American involvement in a possible European war. So did Republicans Robert Taft and Arthur Vandenberg.

So, apparently, did Franklin Roosevelt. "I hate war," the president said in 1936. "I shall pass unnumbered hours, thinking and planning how war may be kept from this nation."[2]

Congress, like the president, appeared to favor neutrality. Laws banned United States ships from war zones and forbade citizens from travelling on belligerent ships. In 1937, Congress instituted a "cash and carry" policy. Foreign belligerent nations could purchase vital products such as oil, steel, or rubber—if they paid in cash and carried them off in their own ships.

Roosevelt, however, saw the dangers of noninvolvement. He asked Congress for increased funds for national defense. Congress refused. He tried to get Congress to rewrite the Neutrality Act after the king and queen of England visited the United States in the summer of 1939. Congress declined to change the act.

While Congress refrained from acting, other countries moved. Germany and Russia signed a five-year nonaggression pact in August 1939. The following month, Germany invaded Poland, and Britain and France declared war on the Germans. World War II had begun.

"This nation will remain a neutral nation," Roosevelt said during a fireside chat on September 3, 1939. He added that he was not asking Americans to be neutral in their thoughts.[3] Roosevelt preached neutrality while secretly following a pro-British course. First, however, there was an election to be won.

"Better a 3rd Termer"

The 1940 presidential election proved to be an unusual one. Franklin D. Roosevelt fought tradition as much as he fought any Republican foe.

Republicans fielded three youthful challengers. Ohio Senator Robert Taft represented the party's conservatives. Thomas Dewey, a New York City prosecutor, won the early primary elections and was the choice of most Americans in polls. Convention delegates, however, chose an unlikely candidate.

Indiana-born Wendell Willkie had never held public office. A Wall Street lawyer and president of a utility company, Willkie was a delegate to the 1924 Democratic convention. The 1939 edition of *Who's Who in America* listed him as a Democrat. Local electric power companies, many of whom feared government companies would put them out of business, were strong Willkie supporters. Willkie secured the Republican nomination on the sixth ballot.

Who would run for the Democrats? Roosevelt, if he ran, would be unbeatable. But if he ran, he would be breaking a 150-year-old tradition. Since the days of George Washington, no American president had served a third term in office. When former President Theodore Roosevelt sought a third nonconsecutive term in 1912, voters rejected him.

Franklin Roosevelt did not announce plans for a third term. At the same time, he did not choose a successor. Secretary of Commerce Harry Hopkins was his closest cabinet ally, but his health ruled him out. Roosevelt's vice president, John Nance Garner, sought the presidency. Roosevelt, who never liked Garner much anyway, refused to support the Texan. James Farley, FDR's postmaster general and former campaign manager, wanted the presidency for himself. His boss refused to recommend him for it.

Roosevelt carried the suspense to the Chicago stadium. Then a groundswell of support for him began. Chicago Mayor Ed Kelly ordered a worker to lead cheers for the president. Suddenly a voice came over the stadium's loudspeakers shouting, "We want Roosevelt! Illinois wants Roosevelt! America wants Roosevelt!" The delegates took up the cry, and Roosevelt swept to the Democratic nomination.

Republicans criticized Roosevelt for seeking to break the two-term tradition. An editorial in the Republican-leaning *Chicago Tribune* commented, "The Democratic convention has nominated for a third term a man who almost established a dictatorship in his second."[4] Democrats countered, "Better a 3rd Termer than a 3rd Rater."[5]

Another factor influenced the election. Germany overran Denmark, Norway, Belgium, and the Netherlands in early 1940. By midsummer, France had fallen. Many Americans felt it was no time to change political leadership.

Roosevelt did not wait for the election to take action on the war. In September 1940, he struck a deal with Britain. The United States delivered fifty World War I-era destroyers to Britain in return for leases to British bases in the Western Hemisphere.

The November vote followed economic lines. Willkie generally did well among middle- and upper-income voters, but Roosevelt swept the low-income votes. Willkie did better against FDR than either Hoover or Landon, but Roosevelt still carried 55 percent of the popular vote.

"Air Raid . . . This Is No Drill"

With the election over, Roosevelt shed any pretense of neutrality. During a December 29 fireside chat, he called for factory owners "to put every ounce of effort into producing . . . munitions swiftly and without stint." Conversion to a wartime economy was vital, he said. "We must be the great arsenal of democracy."[6]

Even before the election, Roosevelt started a military buildup. He authorized twelve billion dollars in defense spending in the summer of 1940—four times as much money as the government had allotted for relief and public works during any preceding year.

Guns and tanks, not consumer goods, rolled off assembly lines. Chrysler spent $33.5 million to build tanks. General Motors and other companies made more than one hundred thousand machine guns. Roosevelt called for the construction of fifty thousand warplanes. Most of these weapons went to the British war effort against Hitler's Nazis. Roosevelt kept the United States out of combat, even after the German navy sank American ships.

However, the military buildup did not bring an instant end to the Depression. More than 5 million people—nearly 10 percent of the workforce—still were unemployed in 1941. That unemployment, however, would not last. Workers began toiling around the clock

This bustling Chicago tractor plant demonstrates the increase in machinery production caused by the upcoming war.

building ships, tanks, and planes. Army bases grew up throughout the country to house soldiers preparing for combat. These bases provided other jobs to nearby residents.

At 8:00 A.M. on December 7, Captain Logan C. Ramsey telegraphed a message: "Air raid . . . Pearl Harbor . . . This is no drill."[7] A tidal wave of more than three hundred fifty Japanese warplanes was shelling America's Pacific fleet at the Hawaii naval base. The Japanese hit eighteen United States ships, destroyed or damaged more than two hundred aircraft, and killed more than twenty-four hundred Americans.

A sign by a courthouse urges young men and women to enlist in the Army. By the time the United States entered World War II, thousands of young men were drafted into the military.

Now there could be no neutrality. The next day Roosevelt declared that "December 7, 1941" was "a date which will live in infamy."[8] Moments later, Congress declared war on Japan. Similar declarations would follow against Germany and Italy.

Thousands of young men and women volunteered for the armed forces after the war declaration. Within months, millions of other young men would be drafted into the military. Any able-bodied adult not in uniform was needed for work in the nation's defense plants. Roosevelt called for seven-day weeks in every war industry, including the production of raw materials. New plants would be built, and old ones enlarged.

The Pearl Harbor raid and the start of World War II helped put an end to the Great Depression. A new, deadlier, and even grimmer challenge now faced Americans.

★ TIMELINE ★

1928—*November:* Republican Herbert Hoover wins presidential election over Democrat Al Smith.

1929—*September 3:* After an up-and-down year, the Dow-Jones industrial average reaches an all-time high of 381.17.

1929—*October 24:* Thousands of stock market small investors lose their life savings during the "Black Thursday" decline. A few major bankers buy stock in a somewhat successful effort to reverse the downturn.

1929—*October 29:* "Black Tuesday," a day of major stock losses, ends without a significant upturn in stock prices. This day is considered the beginning of the Great Depression.

1929—*December:* President Hoover proclaims, "We have re-established confidence," although the Depression will continue throughout the 1930s.

1930—*June:* Hoover signs Smoot-Hawley Act, the highest tariff in American history.

1932—*July 8:* The stock market bottoms out, as the Dow-Jones average plummets to 58.

1932—*July:* Federal troops drive out "Bonus Marchers," World War I veterans seeking a military bonus promised in 1945, from the capital.

1932—*November:* Democrat Franklin D. Roosevelt unseats Hoover in the most one-sided presidential election in sixty-eight years.

1933—*February:* Widespread financial panic causes several states to declare "bank holidays" to stem withdrawals.

1933—*March 4:* Roosevelt is inaugurated and claims, "We have nothing to fear but fear itself."

1933—*March 5:* Roosevelt calls an emergency session of Congress to pass his proposed legislation.

1933—*March 12:* Roosevelt delivers first "fireside chat" to outline plans for his administration.

1933—Roosevelt creates many new government programs, including the Tennessee Valley Authority (TVA), Civil Conservation Corps (CCC), Public Works Administration (PWA), and National Recovery Act (NRA). Chicago celebrates Century of Progress, a fair that attracts 16 million visitors.

1933—Droughts and dust storms create the "dust bowl," causing
–1935 crop failures that lead to thousands of Midwestern farmers losing their land.

1934—Author Upton Sinclair, whose campaign receives worldwide attention, loses election for governor of California.

1935—*May:* Supreme Court strikes down the National Recovery Act (NRA) as unconstitutional.

1935—*September 8:* Louisiana Senator Huey P. Long, a possible 1936 presidential challenger to Roosevelt, is shot to death.

1936—Hitler invades neutral Rhineland and supports Fascist forces in bloody Spanish Civil War.

1936—*August:* Jesse Owens wins four gold medals in Berlin Olympic games.

1936—*November:* Roosevelt wins re-election with greatest landslide in history, carrying every state except Maine and Vermont.

1936—*December:* Workers at the General Motors plant in Flint, Michigan, begin a sit-down strike that leads to a union contract.

1937—*January:* Ohio River floods drown nine hundred people and force half a million more from their homes.

1937—*May:* Police shoot ten strikers and wound one hundred in Chicago's "Memorial Day Massacre."

1937—Roosevelt announces a proposal to add six new justices to the Supreme Court, a move criticized by both Republicans and Democrats as "court packing."

1937—*August:* A recession costs 4 million workers their jobs.

1938—*September:* Allies turn over the western Czechoslovakia region known as the Sudetenland to Hitler.

1938—*November:* Republicans post huge gains in off-year elections.

1939—*September:* Hitler invades Poland, starting World War II.

1939—John Steinbeck publishes *The Grapes of Wrath,* an epic novel about Depression-era migrant workers. The Civil War epic movie *Gone with the Wind* premieres.

1940—*November:* Roosevelt wins an unprecedented third term as president.

1941—*December:* The Japanese bomb the United States naval base at Pearl Harbor, Hawaii, forcing the United States to enter into World War II. The military buildup from the war puts an end to the Depression.

★ CHAPTER NOTES ★

Chapter 1

1. William K. Klingaman, *1929: The Year of the Great Crash* (New York: Harper and Row, 1989), p. 283.
2. Thomas J. Fleming, "Good-bye to Everything," *American Heritage*, vol. 16, no. 5, August 1965, p. 98.
3. Ibid., p. 99.
4. Klingaman, p. 287.
5. Ibid., p. 282.
6. Ibid., p. 285.

Chapter 2

1. William K. Klingaman, *1929: The Year of the Great Crash* (New York: Harper and Row, 1989), p. 58.
2. Robert McElvaine, *The Great Depression: America, 1929–1941* (New York: Times Books, 1993), p. 38.
3. *The Roaring Twenties: 1920–1930* (New York: Time-Life Books, 1970), p. 96.
4. Klingaman, p. 9.
5. McElvaine, p. 14.
6. David Wallechinsky and Irving Wallace, *The People's Almanac* (Garden City, N.Y.: Doubleday, 1975), p. 276.
7. James Patterson, *America in the Twentieth Century* (New York: Harcourt Brace Johanovich, 1976), p. 226.
8. Paul F. Boller, Jr., *Presidential Campaigns* (New York: Oxford University Press, 1984), p. 227.
9. Klingaman, p. 30.
10. Milton Meltzer, *Brother, Can You Spare a Dime?: The Great Depression 1929–1933* (New York: Alfred A. Knopf, 1969), p. 5.
11. Barrington Boardman, *Flappers, Bootleggers, "Typhoid Mary," and the Bomb: An Anecdotal History of the United States from 1923–1945* (New York: Harper and Row, 1989), p. 102.
12. Ibid., p. 103.
13. Klingaman, p. 262.
14. Ibid., p. 266.

Chapter 3

1. Dan Mulvey, ed., *We Had Everything but Money* (Glendale, Wis.: Country Books, 1992), p. 15.
2. Studs Terkel, *Hard Times: An Oral History of the Great Depression* (New York: Pantheon Books, 1986), p. 369.
3. Ibid., p. 5.
4. Ibid., p. xiv.
5. Interview with Carl Lundell, November 26, 1995.
6. Interview with Alice Swanson, November 26, 1995.
7. "Our Century," *U.S. News & World Report*, August 28–September 4, 1995, p. 78.

8. Charles R. Walker, "Relief and Revolution," in *The New Deal: A Documentary History*, ed. William E. Leuchtenberg (New York: Harper Torchbooks, 1968), p. 10.

9. *Hard Times: 1930–1940* (New York: Time-Life Books, 1970), p. 25.

10. William K. Klingaman, *1929: The Year of the Great Crash* (New York: Harper and Row, 1989), p. 313.

11. Lloyd Robinson, *The Hopefuls: Ten Presidential Campaigns* (Garden City, N.Y.: Doubleday and Company, 1966), p. 44.

12. Frederick Lewis Allen, *Since Yesterday: The 1930s in America* (New York: Harper and Row, 1988), p. 27.

13. Ibid., p. 30.

14. Ibid., p. 28.

15. Klingaman, p. 340.

16. Milton Meltzer, *Brother, Can You Spare a Dime?: The Great Depression 1929–1933* (New York: Alfred A. Knopf, 1969), p. 160.

17. Robinson, p. 51.

18. Klingaman, p. 340.

19. Clifton Daniel, ed., *Chronicle of America* (Mt. Kisco, N.Y.: Chronicle Publications, 1989), p. 655.

20. Terkel, p. 16.

21. Allen, p. 102.

Chapter 4

1. Paul F. Boller, Jr., *Presidential Campaigns* (New York: Oxford University Press, 1984), p. 213.

2. Robert S. McElvaine, *The Great Depression: America, 1929–1941* (New York: Times Books, 1993), p. 106.

3. Barrington Boardman, *Flappers, Bootleggers, "Typhoid Mary," and the Bomb: An Anecdotal History of the United States from 1923–1945* (New York: Harper and Row, 1989), p. 143.

4. Boller, p. 231.

5. David Wallechinsky and Irving Wallace, *The People's Almanac* (Garden City, N.Y.: Doubleday, 1975), p. 297.

6. Alex Gottfried, *Boss Cermak of Chicago* (Seattle: University of Washington Press, 1962), p. 325.

Chapter 5

1. Robert S. McElvaine, *The Great Depression: America, 1929–1941* (New York: Times Books, 1973), p. 117.

2. Barrington Boardman, *Flappers, Bootleggers, "Typhoid Mary," and the Bomb: An Anecdotal History of the United States from 1923–1945* (New York: Harper and Row, 1989), p. 151.

3. Ibid.

4. *Franklin Delano Roosevelt Fireside Chats* (New York: Penguin Books, 1995), p. 3.

5. Interview with Ray Cordwell, November 26, 1995.

6. Interview with George Swanson, November 26, 1995.

7. Studs Terkel, *Hard Times: An Oral History of the Great Depression* (New York: Pantheon Books, 1986), p. 115.

8. McElvaine, p. 265.

9. Interview with Marjorie Blakemore, October 26, 1995.

10. Roy Stryker and Nancy Wood, "In This Proud Land," *American Heritage*, vol. 24, no. 5, August 1973, p. 55.

11. Ibid.

12. Hugh Johnson, "The Blue Eagle from Egg to Earth," in *The New Deal: A Documentary History,* ed. William E. Leuchtenberg (New York: Harper Torchbooks, 1968), p. 47.

13. James T. Patterson, *America in the Twentieth Century* (New York: Harcourt Brace Johanovich, 1993), p. 256.

14. Ibid., p. 249.

15. Robert S. McElvaine, ed., *Down and Out in the Great Depression: Letters from the Forgotten Man* (Chapel Hill, N.C.: University of North Carolina Press, 1983), p. 6.

16. McElvaine, *The Great Depression*, p. 229.

17. Patterson, p. 256.

18. McElvaine, *The Great Depression*, p. 349.

19. Terkel, p. 165.

Chapter 6

1. Dan Mulvey, ed., *We Had Everything but Money* (Greendale, Wis.: Country Books, 1992), p. 42.

2. Interview with Ray Cordwell, November 26, 1995.

3. Ibid.

4. Studs Terkel, *Hard Times: An Oral History of the Great Depression* (New York: Pantheon Books, 1986), p. 37.

5. Kenneth Allsop, *Hard Travellin': The Story of the Migrant Worker* (Middlesex, England: New American Library, 1967), p. 114.

6. Nels Anderson, *Men on the Move* (Chicago: University of Chicago Press, 1940), in Allsop, p. 180.

7. Alan Lomax, compiler, *Hard-Hitting Songs for Hard-Hit People* (New York: Oak Publications, 1967), p. 25.

8. Allsop, p. 359.

9. Ibid., p. 363.

10. David Wallechinsky and Irving Wallace, *The People's Almanac* (Garden City, N.Y.: Doubleday, 1975), p. 869.

11. David Wallechinsky and Irving Wallace, *The People's Almanac #2* (New York: Bantam Books, 1978), p. 747.

Chapter 7

1. David Wallechinsky and Irving Wallace, *The People's Almanac* (Garden City, N.Y.: Doubleday, 1975), p. 50.

2. "We Have a Plan," *The Great Depression* produced by Blackside, Inc., (Public Broadcasting Service, 1993).

3. Studs Terkel, *Hard Times: An Oral History of the Great Depression* (New York: Pantheon Books, 1986), p. 316.

4. Frederick Lewis Allen, *Since Yesterday: The 1930s in America* (New York: Harper and Row, 1988), p. 189.

5. *Hard Times: 1930–1940* (New York: Time-Life Books, 1970), p. 162.

6. Robert S. McElvaine, *The Great Depression: America, 1929–1941* (New York: Times Books, 1973), p. 228.

7. Ibid., p. 294.

Chapter 8

1. Robert Houghwout Jackson, *The Struggle for Judicial Supremacy*, quoted in Bernard Schwartz, *A History of the Supreme Court* (New York: Oxford University Press, 1993), p. 233.

2. Frederick Lewis Allen, *Since Yesterday: The 1930s in America* (New York: Harper and Row, 1988), p. 296.

3. Ibid., p. 281.

4. Clifton Daniel, ed., *Chronicle of America* (Mt. Kisco, N.Y.: Chronicle Publications, 1989), p. 681.

Chapter 9

1. Norman H. Finkelstein, *Sounds in the Air: The Golden Age of Radio* (New York: Charles Scribner's Sons, 1993), p. 37.

2. Dan Mulvey, ed., *We Had Everything but Money* (Greendale, Wis.: Country Books, 1992), p. 136.

3. Ann Ellwood, "The Great Martian Invasion," from David Wallechinsky and Irving Wallace, *The People's Almanac #2* (New York: Bantam Books, 1978), p. 44.

4. Ibid., p. 46.

Chapter 10

1. Clifton Daniel, ed., *Chronicle of the Twentieth Century* (New York: Dorling Kindersley Publishing, 1995), p. 485.

2. James T. Patterson, *America in the Twentieth Century* (New York: Harcourt Brace Johanovich, 1993), p. 272.

3. *Franklin Delano Roosevelt Fireside Chats* (New York: Penguin Books, 1995), p. 47.

4. *A Century of Tribune Editorials* (Freeport, N.Y.: Books for Libraries, 1947), p. 124.

5. David Wallechinsky and Irving Wallace, *The People's Almanac* (Garden City, N.Y.: Doubleday Books, 1975), p. 298.

6. *Franklin Delano Roosevelt*, p. 62.

7. Barrington Boardman, *Flappers, Bootleggers, "Typhoid Mary," and the Bomb: An Anecdotal History of the United States from 1923–1945* (New York: Harper and Row, 1989), p. 251.

8. *Great Speeches of the 20th Century*, vol. 2 (Santa Monica, Calif.: Rhino Records, Inc., 1991).

★ FURTHER READING ★

A Century of Tribune Editorials. Freeport, NY: Books for Libraries Press, 1947.

Allen, Frederick Lewis. *Since Yesterday: The 1930s in America*. New York: Harper and Row, 1988.

Allsop, Kenneth. *Hard Travellin': The Story of the Migrant Worker*. Middlesex, England: Penguin Books, 1967.

Boardman, Barrington. *Flappers, Bootleggers, "Typhoid Mary," and the Bomb: An Anecdotal History of the United States from 1923–1945*. New York: Harper and Row, 1989.

Boller, Jr., Paul F., *Presidential Campaigns*. New York: Oxford University Press, 1984.

Csida, Joseph, and June Bunday Csida. *American Entertainment: A Unique History of Popular Show Business*. New York: Billboard Publications, 1979.

Day, Donald. *Will Rogers: A Biography*. New York: David McKay and Company, 1962.

Finkelstein, Norman H. *Sounds in the Air: The Golden Age of Radio*. New York: Charles Scribner's Sons, 1993.

Franklin Delano Roosevelt Fireside Chats. New York: Penguin Books, 1995.

Hard Times: 1930–1940. New York: Time-Life Books, 1969.

Kindleberger, Charles P. *The World in Depression: 1929–1939*. Berkeley: University of California Press, 1986.

Klein, Joe. *Woody Guthrie: A Life*. New York: Alfred A. Knopf, 1980.

Klingaman, William K. *1929: The Year of the Great Crash*. New York: Harper and Row, 1989.

Leuchtenberg, William E., ed. *The New Deal: A Documentary History*. New York: Harper Torchbooks, 1968.

Lomax, Alan, compiler. *Hard-Hitting Songs for Hard-Hit People*. New York: Oak Publications, 1967.

McElvaine, Robert S., ed. *Down and Out in the Great Depression: Letters from the Forgotten Man.* Chapel Hill, NC: University of North Carolina Press, 1983.

McElvaine, Robert S. *The Great Depression: America, 1929–1941.* New York: Times Books, 1984.

Meltzer, Milton. *Brother, Can You Spare a Dime?: The Great Depression 1929–1933.* New York: New American Library, 1969.

Mulvey, Dan, ed. *We Had Everything but Money.* Greendale, WI.: Country Books, 1982.

Official Guide Book of the Fair. Chicago: A Century of Progress, 1934.

Patterson, James T. *America in the Twentieth Century.* New York: Harcourt Brace Johanovich, 1976.

Phillips, Cabell. *From the Crash to the Blitz: 1929–1939.* London: Macmillan, 1969.

Robinson, Lloyd. *The Hopefuls: Ten Presidential Campaigns.* Garden City, N.Y.: Doubleday and Company, 1966.

Steinbeck, John. *The Grapes of Wrath.* New York: Penguin Books U.S.A., 1976.

Stone, Irving. *They Also Ran.* New York: New American Library, 1966.

Terkel, Studs. *Hard Times: An Oral History of the Great Depression.* New York: Pantheon Books, 1986.

The Roaring Twenties: 1920–1930. New York: Time-Life Books, 1969.

Vermilye, Jeremy. *The Films of the Thirties.* Secaucus, NJ: The Citadel Press, 1982.

Wallechinsky, David and Irving Wallace. *The People's Almanac.* Garden City, N.Y.: Doubleday, 1975.

Wallechinsky, David and Irving Wallace. *The People's Almanac #2.* New York: Bantam Books, 1978.

★ INDEX ★